Published by The History Press
Charleston, SC
www.historypress.com

(*Back Cover*) Pike Place Market sign. *Photographs from the Carol M. Highsmith Archive, Library of Congress, Prints and Photographs Division.*

(*Front Cover*) The Smith Tower, located in Pioneer Square, is the oldest skyscraper in Seattle, Washington. *Photographs from the Carol M. Highsmith Archive, Library of Congress, Prints and Photographs Division.*

First published 2020

ISBN 9781540242624

Library of Congress Control Number: 2019954278

Notice: The information in this book is true and complete to the best of our knowledge. It is offered without guarantee on the part of the author or The History Press. The author and The History Press disclaim all liability in connection with the use of this book.

Wicked *Seattle*

TERESA NORDHEIM

THE
History
PRESS

To the men and women of law enforcement
who mark a thin blue line between society and the wicked.

CONTENTS

ACKNOWLEDGEMENTS

𝓔rnest Hemingway once said, "There's nothing to writing. All you do is sit down at a typewriter and open a vein." As a nurse, one might think that I have the key to a hidden lock and that drawing blood is easy for me. That isn't the case. Bringing a historical true crime book to life requires countless hours of time and a lot of energy and patience from both the writer and those closest to them.

It would be impossible to start an acknowledgement section without thanking the two people who loved each other enough to bring me life. Bob and Linda Marsh are two of my biggest supporters. I'm grateful for their presence in my life and will forever cherish our time together.

My daughters, son and granddaughters are my biggest fans and greatest advocates. They are my strength when I feel weak. I love them with every fiber of my being. I want to thank Dalton and Cindi Tune for giving me two wickedly adorable granddaughters, Kaeloni and Gillian Tune. They keep a smile on my face and a warmth in my heart. Katerina Nordheim, どもあ りがと for everything you've given up, allowing me to follow my dream. It hasn't gone unnoticed.

I would also like to thank the Seattle Public Library for graciously allowing me to use many of its wonderful photos. Thank you, Jade D'Addario, for gathering and processing my two pages of requests. I also want to thank Chronicling America for its excellent selection of historical newspapers. To Murray Morgan and William Speidel, I only pray I'm carrying on in your honor to help preserve our area's history, and I'm relentlessly grateful for the hours of work you've contributed to the historical documentation of Seattle, including the good, the bad, the ugly and the wicked cast of characters contained in the pages of this book. Without you, there would be no story.

To my editor, Laurie Krill: Without your kind, caring nature and excellent communication, I may not have written this book. From start to finish, you have encouraged and inspired me.

To my copy editor, Ashley Hill: You helped me perfect the project and kept my spelling in check.

To my mentor, Joe Teeples: Your faith in my abilities, support of my endeavors and kind words of advice inspire me to be a better and more knowledgeable writer.

To my friends, my royal court, Denielle Varnum, Cristin West, Heather Fehr and Tyranni Wells: You're all princesses in my book, and without your emotional support, I might have given up. And Prince Jereza, your karaoke kept me smiling on the hardest of days.

To my publisher, The History Press: Thank you for believing in me, not once, but twice. It's a pleasure to work with you.

WICKED SEATTLE

*S*eattle began with a big bang, or at least a wicked collision, between the Pacific and North American tectonic plates. This fender bender brought Washington above sea level and formed the Cascade Mountain Range. This collision occurred over the course of tens of millions of years, long before there were any human inhabitants on either continent. These mountains, which titivate Washington's topography, continue to act in a wicked fashion, as they are live volcanoes. Fortunately, they have remained calm, apart from a few blasts that sprinkled ash through the state.

As the last ice age (twelve thousand to eighteen thousand years ago) ended, bays, lakes, valleys, hills and ridges formed all around the Pacific Northwest; thus, creating the bizarre terrain that covers the area today. It's this unique atmosphere that brought settlers to the area and still draws people today. Washington is one of the few states which can boast scenery that ranges from ocean beaches to valleys, mountains, deserts, rainforests and volcanoes. The problem with this state lies with its perfect mix of eccentric people; they were both respectable and malicious. The Pacific Northwest is known as the home of many serial killers and the final resting place of their victims. Two of the most notorious killers, Ted Bundy and Gary Ridgway, both came from cities near Seattle and rank among the top twenty most murderous Americans. The area's environment provides copious hiding spots for wild game; its trees provide wealth from lumber, and there is a large amount of fruit to harvest. The Pacific Ocean provides fish and shellfish to feed the hungry.

The area's mountains provide valuable minerals, beauty and entertainment, its rainforests provide tropical foods and animals that may not otherwise tolerate the Pacific Northwest's cold climate and its valleys have rich soil for crops and livestock. The good things about the area outweigh the bad, but the bad things are ever present. There are ample places to hide dead bodies, keep out of the public eye and make enough money to bring trouble to the front doorstep.

Located in the Pacific Northwest, Washington is currently the eighteenth-largest state in the continental United States. Named in honor of the nation's first president, George Washington, Washington was admitted to the United States late in the country's history. Out of the nation's fifty states, Washington was the forty-second, admitted on November 11, 1889, but its history had been forged much earlier. Seattle is a seaport city in Washington and is the largest city in the state. It took Seattle many years to reach its current population, which totals well over 700,000 people, but wasn't long after the wicked collision that the state's first inhabitants began to stumble into the area and explore the land.

Before the arrival of white settlers, Washington and the area that is now known as Seattle was home to a variety of Native American tribes; the Native Americans who explored the area found much to love. The Duwamish tribe built permanent longhouses along the Duwamish River. The waters of the area provided fish and shellfish, and the lands provided copious amounts of berries, an assortment of wildlife, fertile soil for planting and acres of farmland for livestock, which were used for food and clothing. The natives were content with their lives in the Pacific Northwest until European explorers and settlers began to arrive. There were battles between the white settlers and the natives, and the early battles created tension and turmoil. The settlers were fighting for land that wasn't theirs to take, while the natives were fighting to protect the land they loved and called home. While these battles took place hundreds of years ago, people are still reminded of the region's native heritage every time they say the name Seattle.

The tale of the founding of Seattle by white settlers can vary depending on the storyteller or historian. Most agree that fishing, lumber and gold drew settlers to the area. Again, the climate, terrain and abundance of sustainable food provided by the land and sea also encouraged settlers to remain in Seattle. Coffee, computers and airplanes came much later in the city's history.

The true founders of Seattle were the Native American tribes who covered the land, but it was the white settlers who brought people, constructed sawmills and built a thriving city. Explorers stumbled into Washington

A view of early Seattle's streets and buildings. *Courtesy of Seattle Municipal Archives.*

in 1775, when Captain Bruno Heceta claimed the land for Spain. Later, more European explorers arrived, including two famous British captains; Captain James Cook arrived in 1778, and George Vancouver arrived in 1792. Vancouver traveled around Puget Sound and claimed settlements and waterways for Britain. American captain Robert Gray arrived to explore the region around the same time as Vancouver; Gray was responsible for naming the Columbia River. Each explorer marked his way by leaving a few reminders of his name or the names of close friends and relatives. Seattle still didn't have a name or any permanent residents, aside from the Native Americans. There are at least two stories about the founding of Seattle and one about how the city received its name.

The first and most popular story of the arrival of Seattle's first settlers is that of the Denny Party, which scouted the area in September 1851. When the Denny Party arrived at Alki Point, near Seattle, in November 1851, it had been over fifty years since the first explorer had come to Washington. Those familiar with Washington weather would agree that this story could begin with, "On a dark and stormy night..."; odds are, rain was falling, and storm clouds were brewing at Alki Point on the night of the Denny Party's arrival. The names of people in this group prominently decorate the street signs of modern Seattle. The leader, Arthur Denny, left Cherry Grove, Illinois, in April 1851. The original party included Arthur's father, stepmother and two older brothers, who all ultimately settled in Oregon. Arthur's younger brother, David, also came along. Arthur also brought his wife, Mary Ann Boren, and her siblings, Louisa and Carson Boren.

Arthur Armstrong Denny was born on June 20, 1822, in Indiana. The Denny family resided in Illinois throughout Arthur's childhood. His early years were quite difficult and filled with daily challenges. He spent much of his time caring for his invalid mother and could only attend school part time, but his determination was strong. He didn't let the faults in his life hold him back from achieving success. He learned carpentry, taught school and studied surveying; Arthur even became a civil engineer. He made the decision to travel west in order to provide a better life for himself and for his family. The journey was one of the hardest obstacles that Denny had ever tackled, and it didn't help that he was ill for much of the journey. Thankfully, he remained strong enough to lead the party to each destination and through each struggle. The party met John Low along the way, and he joined them for the rest of the trip.

The Denny Party arrived in Portland, Oregon, in July 1851. Mary Denny, who had been pregnant throughout the journey, gave birth to Rolland Denny on September 2, 1851. The party needed time to recover and protect the newborn, so they remained in Portland. David Denny and John Low, however, traveled north to explore the area around the Puget Sound. There, they met Leander Terry in the newly founded city of Olympia. In the city, they also met Michael Simmons, the wealthy founder of Tumwater. Terry guided the men to Alki Point, suggested that they make a settlement in the area and helped David construct a cabin. The men were helped along by the local Native Americans. David was in poor health, and he severely injured his foot while using an axe, so he remained in Alki while Low returned to Portland to retrieve the remaining party.

Meanwhile, in Portland, Arthur recruited three new members for their party. He met Nathaniel Bell; his wife, Sarah; and Charlie Terry, who happened to be the younger brother of Leander. In November 1851, the Denny party left Portland via the schooner *Exact*, which was bound for the Puget Sound. The trip was difficult, as Arthur became quite ill and struggled to continue north. When they arrived at Alki, Arthur was greeted by his brother David, who had an ominous message, "I wish you hadn't

Left: A portrait of Seattle's founding father, Arthur Armstrong Denny. *Courtesy of Seattle Public Library.*

Below: A drawing of the first cabin for the Denny Party, located at Alki Point. *Courtesy of Seattle Municipal Archives.*

An early view of Seattle's streets and buildings at Pike Place Market. *Courtesy of Seattle Public Library.*

come." Winter was approaching, and Leander Terry and John Low had already staked claims in Alki. The Denny Party completed the cabin that had been started by David and Terry, and they settled in to wait for the harsh winter to pass. After the worst of winter cleared, the party explored the north, south, east and west before they finally settled on an island near Elliott Bay; the site is now called Pioneer Square and is located in the heart of present-day Seattle.

It is at this point that the second tale of Seattle's founding comes into play. David "Doc" Maynard became Arthur Denny's rival on various levels. Historians agree that Maynard held a large stake in the founding of the city. However, he and Arthur Denny were as different as night and day; most importantly, Maynard wasn't always as reputable. He had several vices that tarnished his appearance in the public and forced many to see him in a wicked light. Maynard was born in Vermont on March 22, 1808, and his upbringing appears to have been much less complicated than Denny's. Maynard was accepted to medical school at the age of seventeen; he was intelligent and graduated at the top of his class. He married Lydia Rickey in 1828, and the couple later had a daughter and a son. In 1832, the Maynard family moved to Ohio. There, Maynard attempted to build a medical school and enter both political and business ventures. His good luck and intelligence, however, did not prevail this round, as he failed on all accounts. Maynard's easy start to life began to take a turn for the worse. By 1850, he had lost a small fortune and learned that his wife had been unfaithful. He became a humbled man and turned to alcohol to ease the stressors in his life.

Rather than sticking around to deal with his shortcomings, Maynard decided that it was time to move on to bigger and better escapades. He left his family in Ohio and allowed Lydia to file for divorce and start a new life without him. He ventured to California and eventually found himself in the Puget Sound area. Along the way, Maynard met and fell in love with Catherine Broshears, the sister of Michael Simmons. Their love did not sit well with Simmons, who believed his sister deserved only the best of suitors—perhaps he knew that Maynard was still married. Although Maynard expected Lydia to end their marriage, she had never filed for divorce. Maynard reached the social status of an adulterer. It could have been the friendship held between Simmons and Arthur Denny that influenced Simmons's choice to accept Maynard into his family tree, as he wanted to introduce Denny and Maynard.

In 1852, Maynard claimed a tract of 640 acres of land in the same area as Arthur Denny's settlement. He hired natives to help build a cabin and a general store. He had his eye on expanding, but Carson Boren had already claimed the land to the south. The remains of the land disputes and surveys of Boren, Denny and Maynard are still visible in the layout of the streets of Seattle. The city doesn't have nice blocks, which can been seen in an average city; instead, Seattle's streets are slanted. Maynard's general store became a hub of centralized activity, and he became the first justice of the peace—not bad for a small-town doctor from Vermont.

Maynard was older than most of the settlers in the area, and his distinct character helped him see things from a different point of view—he was a worthy rival to Denny. By the time Maynard arrived in Seattle, he had already assisted in the development of a city in Ohio, so he had more experience than Denny when it came to city planning. Maynard liked to drink liquor, which was opposed by most members of the Denny Party. Maynard's friend Captain Leonard Felker even found a woman to start a brothel: the infamous Madame Damnable. Maynard believed that vice was a valid part of a frontier town.

It was Maynard's down-to-earth political and negotiation skills that helped him defuse the difficult situations that kept arising between the white settlers and the local natives of the Duwamish tribe. He had a friendship with the

Above: Catherine Maynard sitting next to Doc Maynard's grave at Lake View Cemetery. *Courtesy of Seattle Public Library.*

Right: Chief Seattle closed his eyes in this photo, as he believed the camera could capture his soul. *Courtesy of Seattle Public Library.*

tribal leaders and their members, which eased the growing concerns of the natives. Without Maynard or his bond with the natives, Seattle may have been called Denny. Instead, Seattle is one of the few major cities that was named in honor of a Native American chief. Maynard played a key role in naming the new city and chose to name it after his good friend. He pushed to name the settlement after the leader of the Duwamish and Snohomish tribes, Chief Si'ahl or Sealth (pronounced "See-ahis"). This name was difficult for English speakers and was later changed to Seattle, which flows off the tongue with ease.

So, was it the respectable Arthur Denny or the questionable Doc Maynard who truly founded Seattle? Both men played vital roles in building the city, and they each contributed in building one of the greatest cities on the West Coast. What the two men couldn't have predicted was the wild and wicked ride the city took as it forged its way in the world.

DEFIANCE OF UNLAWFUL AUTHORITY

Governor Isaac Stevens

*I*saac Ingalls Stevens was born on March 24, 1818, to Isaac and Hannah Stevens, in Andover, Massachusetts. His descendants had lived in Massachusetts for years and were among the first settlers in the Massachusetts Bay Colony. Some historians believe he suffered from a form of dwarfism, due to his small stature; however, Stevens's size didn't stop him from accomplishing big things in his life. His extreme intelligence and ambition gave him enough grit to achieve goals that most men can only dream of.

Stevens started his education at the Phillips Academy in Andover, Massachusetts. This boarding school, which opened in 1778, offers university preparatory classes for students between the ninth and twelfth grades. The school also provides a postgraduate year for those who wish to seek further education. The school is highly selective, and only around 13 percent of applicants are accepted; not only was Stevens accepted, but he also excelled in his schooling. This historic school is still in operation today.

Upon graduating from the Phillips Academy, Stevens entered the United States Military Academy at West Point, New York. Established in 1802, West Point Academy is one of the four military service academies in the United States and is known worldwide as one of the most prestigious educational systems for those seeking a military career. Again, Stevens excelled during his time at the academy. He was a capable learner and graduated first in his class in 1839. He majored in mathematics, engineering, surveying, military strategy and politics. After graduating from West Point, Stevens obtained a job with the impressive Army Corps of Engineers, where he served for several years and showed off his talent for engineering and planning. Through this job, Stevens assisted with the building of Fort Adams, which was part of the first system of coastal fortification built by the United States. He also helped with the construction of Fort Knox, which once housed most of the United States' gold reserves. Stevens was ultimately promoted to first lieutenant for his accomplishments; he achieved this rank only one year after graduating from West Point Academy.

Stevens continued to serve with the Corp of Engineers through the Mexican-American War; there, he had his first taste of combat. He received a promotion to captain and led his troops into the Battle of Chapultepec. From there, Stevens received another brevet promotion to major. He came out of the battle with severe injuries but continued to fly through the ranks and add medals to his already well-embellished uniform.

Through several battles, the United States continued to acquire new territories that needed to be mapped and clearly defined. Stevens joined the newly established United States Coast and Geodetic Survey; this agency determines and manages a national coordinate system that provides the foundation for transportation and communication. Joining this agency brought Isaac Stevens to Washington.

Stevens supported Democrat Franklin Pierce's run for president in 1852. He agreed with Pierce's wish to fulfill Manifest Destiny, or the idea that the United States was destined to stretch from the East Coast to the West Coast. Stevens's active support during Pierce's campaign helped jumpstart his political career. He sent his application to become the governor of the Washington Territory to the fourteenth president. This position also carried the title of superintendent of Indian affairs. Stevens's ambitious nature wouldn't allow him to be satisfied with only two titles, so he petitioned to hold a third title. He asked to have a job with the transcontinental railroad survey and took command of the survey for the northern route. The railroad was one of the most popular upcoming attractions in the United States and was at the forefront of everyone's mind.

Stevens left for the Washington Territory in June 1853. He and his crew were responsible for the documentation of a potential railroad route, the flora and fauna in the area and the region's Native American tribes. The group reached Fort Vancouver on November 19, 1853. Though it took four years to complete, the survey was the most complete of those that were submitted for consideration to be a railroad route to the Pacific. Without the railroad's arrival in Washington, Seattle may have remained a small coastal port.

Pioneer Square. *Courtesy of Seattle Municipal Archives.*

Congress declared Washington a territory in March 1853, and Isaac Stevens assumed his official post as the first governor of the area on November 25, 1853. When he arrived at the Washington Hotel in Olympia, Washington, there was a bit of confusion. Stevens wasn't allowed to enter the building until the governor arrived, but upon proper identification, he began his official duties. Until that point, Stevens had proven himself to be an intelligent man, a worthy engineer and a real asset to the new territory. However, there are two sides to every story, and often, there are two sides to a person's personality. Out of nowhere, an evil side peeked its head out of Stevens's personality, and an adventure began.

The Native Americans of the Pacific Northwest weren't pleased with the new influx of white settlers. Areas with prairies, those beside riverbanks and coastal lands were granted to the settlers, and Native Americans were pushed away from the most desirable and sustainable regions. Stevens chose to divide the territory into districts and assigned an agent to each zone. The agents were told to find representatives from each local tribe and work on drawing up treaties. Stevens didn't stick around to help or see how the agreements played out; instead, he left for Washington, D.C., to negotiate for more funding for the railroad and land improvements in his territory. He knew that the railroad would make a lot of money for the state, so it became the top priority.

Stevens returned to Washington with his wife and children in December 1854. The situation between the natives and the settlers had not improved; in fact, it was worse. The agents were making rounds and selecting Native American representatives from each tribe, but there were many stumbling blocks, including language barriers. Sadly, the natives found themselves in a position where they either had to adapt to the settlers' new ways or move out of the area. The treaties were difficult to negotiate, as the language barriers and desires for the land got in the way of fair settlements.

Between December 25, 1854, and February 26, 1855, Stevens organized four meetings to discuss treaties. Each of these sessions lasted for four days. Stevens's overall goal was to gather all Native Americans onto one reservation, which would leave all of the land available for development by white settlers. Rather than seeing the Native Americans as belonging to

Washington State Governor's Mansion, current day. *Courtesy of Washington State Digital Archives.*

nearly thirty individual tribes, the settlers recognized them as belonging one race and tribe. Because of this, the settlers saw no reason to have more than one reservation of land for these individuals. Tribes with different languages and cultures were clumped together as one. One tribe allowed Stevens to make one binding treaty, with very basic wording, to cover all four meetings. The deals were written in one primary language, and the only interpretations came from tribal leaders who could read both native and English languages. The negotiations used Chinook Jargon, which was primarily used for pidgin trade in the Pacific Northwest. Such language was simple and allowed two or more groups that didn't have a common language to communicate through words, sounds and body language. While Chinook Jargon was typical, not all Native American tribes could communicate using it. It was also such a simple language that much of its meaning became lost when it was put into difficult legal terms.

The settlers wanted to be free and clear—they didn't want to owe anything to the Native Americans. To keep them away, the government bribed the Native Americans with items such as food and clothing. The treaties allowed Native Americans to hunt and fish in the places they knew; they also allowed them to gather berries and roots for their food supply. Native Americans were permitted to construct temporary huts for drying their fish and pasturing their horses on unclaimed lands. However, they could not reside in their usual territories or roam free, as the reservation confined them to one area.

The first of the treaties was negotiated at Medicine Creek. The area is near a stream known as She-nah-nam; the name refers to a sacred place where shamans go to get their spiritual power from water. While translators from nearly every distinct tribe were present, Stevens refused to use anything but Chinook Jargon. He felt that the Native Americans could not have access to any area that contained good farmland or any space that the railroad might travel through. Good land would have provided Native Americans with bountiful crops and money from the railroad, which Stevens wanted to remain in the hands of the white settlers. He didn't want to lose his power over the Native Americans.

Chief Leschi represented the Nisqually tribe as their subchief and immediately showed his distaste for the treaty. He insisted on keeping his homeland and wanted to make sure that the deal was in the best interest of both parties. He declined to sign the treaty and left Medicine Creek, refusing to return. Some of the chiefs signed the treaties, while others rejected. Even though Chief Leschi had departed with no intent to sign, his name appeared on the documents.

The Treaty of Point Elliot ended in much the same manner. Again, a few of the eighty-two chiefs signed, and some refused. Those who did sign were thought to have done so under duress. Chief Sealth, the chief of the Duwamish and Suquamish, signed the treaty, but it's unknown whether he signed of his free will or under pressure. The signing of the Treaty of Point No Point was halted when two chiefs demanded extra time to go over the treaties with the members of their tribes. But in the end, all of the chiefs' signatures appeared on the contract. Many historians believe that these, too, were forged by the governor, who was eager to end the negotiations. Some of the chiefs' signatures were marked with an "X" rather than their name. After several more rounds of negotiations, it became clear that Governor Stevens wasn't going to get the outcome he desired. Enraged, he threatened the Native American tribes and told them that he would call in the military if they didn't cooperate with him. By June 1855, the treaties were all signed—in one form or another.

Native Americans were confined to several reservations. One victory for the Native Americans, however, was that white settlers were not allowed on the reservation. Despite this, many white miners found it easier to take shortcuts through the reservations, and along the way, they stole horses and abused Native American women. The Native Americans didn't tolerate this betrayal; the Yakima tribe responded by killing miners. On September 20, 1855, Agent Andrew Bolon of the Bureau of Indian Affairs was sent out to investigate the deaths of the miners. He met with Chief Shumaway from the Yakima tribe, who warned him that the guilty party was much too dangerous to confront, and he advised Bolon to turn around and head home. Bolon heeded his advice but didn't make it to safety before meeting his death at the hands of Chief Shumaway's son, Mosheel, who stabbed him in the throat with a knife. Chief Shumaway responded to Bolon's murder by immediately sending a representative to speak with military officials. He knew this act would create tension, and his method of dealing with the murder set a precedent for future encounters. Chief Shumaway also called for the arrest of his son; Shumaway intended to turn him over to the territorial government in the hopes of avoiding a confrontation. The chief was a wise man, however, and still prepared his men for battle. This was a valid move, as the territorial government had already sent troops to attack the tribe and avenge the death of their agent. Thus, the Yakima War began.

Chief Leschi was half Nisqually and half Yakima; he allied himself with the Yakima tribe and sent warriors to battle. On October 30, 1855, Leschi's warriors ambushed seven men who were representatives of the territorial government. Two of those men, A. Benton Moses and Joseph Miles, were killed. Almost a year later, Governor Stevens lowered the hammer and requested that federal troops charge five Native American men in the deaths of the two representatives. One of the men charged was Chief Leschi, who was the tribal leader. Federal troops had made peace with Chief Leschi when he admitted defeat and fled to the Cascades, but Governor Stevens held a grudge and demanded Leschi's capture. He offered a reward of fifty blankets for any information that could lead to Leschi's arrest. Leschi turned himself over and was to be delivered to Captain Ford by his nephew in the early morning hours of November 13, 1856; he was delivered to the governor the following day. Leschi's brother turned himself in but was killed by an unknown assailant while being held in the governor's office the night before his trial. Leschi went on trial for murder on November 17, 1856, in Steilacoom, Washington. Governor Stevens knew that if the people found Leschi guilty of murder, then he would be declared a hero and strong leader. If Leschi was found innocent, however, then Stevens could be discredited and censured by his military and political counterparts. He was determined to do everything in his power to seal Leschi's fate; the treaties had been detrimental to the governor's public image.

The original court records were destroyed in a fire, but historians and witnesses shared enough details to keep the history books updated. Ezra Meeker, the founder of Puyallup, Washington, told his version of the history in his memoir; he was one of the jurymen for the trial. In his memoir, Meeker spoke of Governor Stevens's eccentric actions, and he stated that the governor had a willingness to shed the blood of innocent citizens to prove his point. Meeker was not alone in his opinions of the cruel actions that took place during Chief Leschi's trial. Others came forward to defend Leschi. During a secret ballot of the twelve jurymen, a group that included many well-known pioneers, eight voted to convict Leschi and four opposed. Judge Chevoweth stated that if the deed was carried out as an act of war, then the prisoner could not be held liable to civil law. When the jury entered the court, they asked for dismissal, as they were unable to agree. However, their request was denied, and the men returned to their negotiations. Finally, two jury members were swayed; Ezra Meeker and William Kinkaid, the founder of Sumner, Washington, refused to change their votes. Thanks to these two men and their determination, Chief Leschi had a hung jury and lived for a few more months while he waited for a second trial.

On March 18, 1857, Chief Leschi had a second trial. This time, the hearing was moved to Olympia, Washington. At the time, the City of

Ezra Meeker's mansion in Puyallup, Washington. *Author's collection.*

The home of Isaac Stevens, Washington's first territorial governor. *Courtesy of Washington State Digital Archives.*

Olympia favored the governor and disliked Native Americans. Presided over by Judge Lander, the jury received many different instructions. They were asked to find Leschi guilty whether they believed he was guilty of the murders or assisted with the murders. So, the jury convicted Chief Leschi of murder and sentenced him to death by hanging on June 10, 1857. An appeal came nine months later, and again, the verdict was guilty, and the punishment was death by hanging. His execution date was moved to January 22, 1858, before it was moved once more to February 1858. At fifty years old, Chief Leschi was hanged at the gallows near Lake Steilacoom on February 19, 1858. Stevens believed that he came out the victor in Leschi's trial, but many thought he encouraged the hanging of an innocent man,

Isaac Stevens secured a commission as a brigadier general of volunteers when the Civil War broke out in 1861. He was killed in action during the Battle of Chantilly on September 1, 1862. Governor Stevens made the news in Washington again on December 10, 2004. Nearly 146 years after the execution, the courts exonerated Chief Leschi through a unanimous vote of the Historical Court of Inquiry.

OPERATING A HOUSE
OF ILL REPUTE

John Pinnell

*L*ocating historical information on John Pinnell (sometimes spelled Pennell) is a struggle. History books often focus on people who are memorable for their prestigious contributions to society. Pinnell played a key role in the history of Seattle, despite the nature of his business. Many have tried to hide his contributions, but he brought an overabundance of money to the area, played a vital role in the railroad business and saved part of the city from a financial depression during a time of panic. Often, members of the public will sweep under the rug what they don't want to see.

When conducting research for this book, it was disappointing to learn that a prolific Northwest historian had passed away before publishing her book on John Pinnell. Ruby McAndrew, who wrote under her maiden name, Ruby El Hult, left behind an unfinished manuscript that profiled the life and times of Pinnell when she passed away at the age of ninety-five in 2008. Pinnell also appears in the insightful writings of the great Bill Speidel and Murray Morgan, and he has a few rare mentions on websites.

Seattle boomed early with mining, fishing and logging, which provided a lot of jobs. These weren't occupations in which the women of the time thrived. The Washington Territory was rapidly occupied by single men who had money in their pockets and time on their hands. Respectable women who were looking to settle down and start a family wanted nothing to do with the cold, dreary and male-dominated Pacific Northwest. In Seattle's early years, only one out of ten of the adults in the region were female, and almost every girl over the age of fifteen quickly became engaged due to the unbalanced ratio. This shortage of women presented a huge problem, and many Seattleites were eager to rectify the situation. After all, the city would never be able flourish if it didn't have families who would reproduce and leave behind heirs.

Asa Mercer desired to make Seattle a thriving city. He is mostly remembered as a founder and the first president of the University of Washington, which he opened with the help of his brothers. The brothers cleared the land and constructed the university; as soon as construction was complete, Mercer— the only college graduate in town—became the school's first instructor and president. The University of Washington provided higher education for residents of the Pacific Northwest, and it assisted in building strong and influential citizens. The city lacked young people seeking degrees, and Mercer noted that employed men outnumbered those who needed schooling. While it didn't take a college degree to see that the area was greatly lacking women, Mercer was one of the first to take action and make a change for the future. Others viewed soliciting woman for marriage as iniquitous.

In 1864, through private funding, Mercer raised enough money to travel to the eastern states and search for women who were willing to work as teachers or dressmakers and in other respectable occupations in the Pacific Northwest. He knew that the men of Seattle were making money and thriving, but they were missing one required item: companionship. The Civil War was ending in the East, and many women and children were left behind when their husbands and fathers perished in battle. The deaths of these men left women who were willing to go to the West and start a new life with a new husband. Mercer needed a way to encourage the young women to travel back to Seattle.

In 1864, Mercer began his journey to the East. He had previously arranged for married couples in Seattle to host the young women he brought home. During this era, some felt that there was a touch of wickedness in the business of importing women; they felt that it was "unsavory" and wrong. In those days, it was usually thought that a woman traveling without a companion had ulterior motives and worked in an insalubrious profession. Respectable women remained under the watchful eyes of their fathers, brothers and husbands. The governor of the Washington Territory supported Mercer's action but could not offer money to help him on his endeavor. It never sat well with the public to support such an undertaking.

Upon reaching Boston, Mercer took to the stage, after a worthy introduction, and attempted to sell his idea to the townspeople. The locals weren't sure about how to receive Mercer's proposal; they didn't know that he

Founded by the Mercer brothers, the University of Washington remains a pillar in the Seattle area. *Courtesy of Seattle Public Library.*

was one of the founders and the president of the University of Washington. Mercer didn't disclose his status in Seattle to the Bostonian strangers before him. The people of Boston knew him as a stranger who had traveled from the opposite side of the United States to beg them to send their available women to the bachelors in Seattle. Each woman needed $250 to pay for her passage from New York to Seattle. Some of the single men in Seattle paid this fee, but not all of them could afford to send money. While many women were eager to travel with Mercer, most of them could not come up with the money they need to travel.

Mercer left New York Harbor with eight women and one man on a cold day in March 1864. The one man who was traveling with them was the father of two of the young women, and he had been ill. He felt that a climate change could improve his poor health, and he wanted to ensure that his daughters had a safe journey and better lives. The group picked up three more passengers in Massachusetts; another woman paid the fare to board but intended to part ways upon their arrival in San Francisco, California. During the journey, she changed her mind and ultimately decided to travel to Seattle with Mercer. The group arrived in Seattle on May 16, 1864. Considerable fanfare had been planned but did not occur. Due to the late hour of their arrival, the group was greeted by only a few locals. The women went to a hotel for the night. The next day, they traveled to the university, where they were properly introduced to the townspeople and their host families. While the entire process may have been odd, it was essential in keeping Seattle afloat.

This first expedition wasn't nearly as prosperous as Mercer had anticipated, so he promptly began planning a second voyage. He planned to leave for New York on January 16, 1866, and he hoped to return to Seattle with seven hundred unmarried women on May 28, 1866. He returned from his second trip with thirty-four women, which was more than he had returned with the first time, but it was far fewer than the seven hundred he intended. Mercer did, however, find his wife on this second voyage. He was instantly smitten with Annie Stephens, but it took her a bit longer to warm up to Mercer. He told her, before their arrival in Seattle, that he intended to marry her, but she declined his offer. Eventually, she broke down and married him on July 15, 1866.

Mercer's efforts brought several teachers, seamstresses and wives to Seattle, but the area's population was still heavily male. If the town couldn't find a way to keep its young men out of trouble and entertained, it would have to move them out to other populated areas, such as San Francisco, California. But that same California city brought a man to the area who could help. He had been running a successful business in San Francisco, a business that provided entertainment for single men—at a price.

A grave for one of the many Mercer girls, who came to Seattle to find a new home and help balance the low female population. *Author's collection.*

In 1861, John Pinnell introduced Seattle to the world of brothels. Brothels provided men the opportunity to rent a room, where a woman could sexually—or otherwise—entertain them. Without the constraints of married life, men could pay for a few moments of companionship. The degree of naughtiness depended only on the man's desires and his bank account. The brothel itself was a large rectangular building, constructed from rough boards by Pinnell. It didn't matter how bejeweled the exterior of the building appeared; it was the women inside who brought in the customers. Inside, the building held a small dance floor, a long bar and several small, private rooms, where the real business transactions took place. The brothel's flooring was nothing more than sawdust from the Yesler Mill. Though many of Seattle's first settlers—like those from the Denny Party—were opposed to this new vice's arrival in town, Pinnell promised to only conduct his business near the mill, which was often referred to as the Tenderloin, Skid Row or Lava Beds.

Henry Yesler couldn't have known his business would become the centerpiece of Seattle's sinners when he contributed to Seattle's history by building a steam-powered mill in late March 1853. The heavily forested areas in the Washington Territory provided the wood that was needed to build Seattle, the surrounding cities and even much of San Francisco. The mill stood on the eastern shore of Elliott Bay and was adjacent to what is now Yesler Way. The term "Skid Row" is now commonly used to describe typically impoverished and urban areas that are inhabited by those who are "on the skids," the poor, homeless and forgotten individuals within society. The term originates from Seattle; the road leading from Yesler Mill to the waterways was the original Skid Row. The mill sat on a hill, and the logs would skid down the road to the water below—the logs would travel down Skid Row. When the company fired a logger, people would say that he was "sent down the skid road." At the heart of Seattle's Skid Row sat John Pinnell's brothel.

The seedy side of Seattle was growing and quickly became filled with gambling clubs, cribs, salons and box houses. It was an area for entertainment that carried on into the late hours of the night—every night—and police officers often looked the other direction when they witnessed illegal activity. Pinnell called his business Illahee, which, when loosely translated, means "home place" or "home away from home" in the native jargon.

The United States Census Bureau's records from 1870 indicate that Pinnell had eleven women working in his establishment. The first women who worked for Pinnell were Native Americans; he went to tribal leaders

Seattle's totem pole in Pioneer Square is a symbol of the city's history. *Courtesy of Seattle Municipal Archives.*

and offered a trade of supplies to families who sent their young female family members to work in his brothel. Pinnell bartered with food, blankets, items of clothing and other goods that were needed by the tribes. The women and their families were more than happy to accept his offer.

Pinnell was a wise businessman who knew how to get what he wanted. Long before he built his establishment or recruited any women, Pinnell went to the men in charge of Seattle and offered them a yearly fee of $1,000 to $1,200 for the privilege of operating his business near the mill. This fee allowed him to conduct his business without any threat from local law enforcement and city officials.

Before Pinnell, prostitution in Seattle had been much more casual and discreet. Boats coming into the Puget Sound, filled with sailors, would be greeted by women who were willing to entertain them for a price. The number of these women varied, and they needed a location to have their affairs in private. The Illahee provided structure and year-round availability to those who sought company. It also provided the City of Seattle with an income, which helped keep the town afloat during financially rough years. Some of the original settlers considered fighting to close the Illahee, but Pinnell had enough pull with the politicians in charge and hush money to keep his business going strong.

During this time, Seattle was also battling for the Northern Pacific Railway to choose the city as the hub for the new intercontinental connection. Pinnell attempted to start a subsidiary brothel in Tacoma, but the railroad kicked him out after a homicide occurred at the location. He continued to build and promote his Seattle location and hoped that the flock of visitors would attract the attention of the railroad officials. Part of Pinnell's business strategy involved him traveling back to San Francisco to recruit white girls, whom he moved back to Seattle to live alongside the Native American girls who were already working for him. Thus, he was able to offer a wider variety of women to his customers, and this made him more competitive the newer brothels that were starting to sprinkle the area.

In 1869, Pinnell had an idea for a second business and built Seattle's first automobile racetrack. The mile-long racetrack was in operation for nine years; today's Meadows horse-racing track was built just south of this location and is still in operation today. It's possible that Pinnell chose the wrong vehicle to race. Had he wanted to race horses, this industry may have added to the gambling that still takes place today.

The popularity of Illahee eventually rivaled that of its competitors in California, and it indeed attracted attention. The brothel also started the notorious box houses, which offered gambling, liquor and entertainment of many varieties. Not everyone appreciated the influx of money and vices into the city; at least one citizen wrote to the newspaper pleading with anyone who would listen. The writer pointed out that the schoolhouse stood near

The first courthouse in the area, where Chief Leschi's first trial was held. *Courtesy of Washington State Digital Archives.*

the Illahee, and they also noted the number of young families in the area. They also indicated that such a house—"a pest house" or "madhouse"— would attract infectious diseases that could spread to the youth in the area. The writer may have been onto something; by 1877, smallpox hit the Illahee hard and created fear among the area's locals. Shortly after this epidemic, Pinnell began to lose interest in his business and decided that he had earned more than enough money to retire comfortably.

In May 1878, the old Pinnell brothel caught fire and disappeared into the shadows of history. Between thirty and forty homes and buildings were lost in the fire, and it was reported that the smoke was visible from Tacoma and Port Townsend. The mayhem of the fire made it easy for Pinnell to walk away from Seattle and his business in order to retire in Eastern Washington with his wife, Annie. When he left Seattle, Pinnell had between $40,000 and $50,000 to his name. The money was a fair sum to retire with; he lived peacefully on a beautiful farm near Ellensburg, where he spent the rest of his years raising horses and cattle. On the night of February 2, 1883, Pinnell reportedly died from a sudden illness brought on by heart disease. His name faded from the newspapers, but his mark on the city's history remained.

PROFANITY IN
THE SEVENTH DEGREE

Mother Damnable

*L*ong before the arrival of Boeing, Microsoft, Amazon and Starbucks, the Pacific Northwest came to life as a timber and seafood port. Young, single men moved to the area to work in the mines, log the evergreen forests and fish the waters of the Puget Sound. The lush forestry in Washington provided enough wood to supply many of the cities along the West Coast. Much of the wood that was sold from Washington was processed and cut at Yesler's Mill before it was sold and shipped to San Francisco and other coastal towns. The money that was made from timber sales helped build the city of Seattle. The first homes and buildings in Seattle and the surrounding area were constructed from home-grown timber. The Pacific Ocean and the area's rivers and bays provided enough fish to feed the locals and supply local trade.

The Pacific Northwest offered an abundance of natural resources, but there was one essential resource that was scarce in the region. In 1869, men in Seattle outnumbered women nine to one. Asa Mercer attempted to recruit women from the East, and by 1890, the ratio of men to women was only two to one. With this tilted variable and limited access to social activities, a few of the well-known women in Seattle started to provide their own entertainment. Crib houses, box houses and brothels quickly populated the area, and sin seeped its way into Seattle. What John Pinnell started, the women of Seattle took over and ran with even more vigor.

The first woman to venture into the brothel business was Mary Ann Conklin—also known as Mother Damnable and Madame Damnable.

Conklin was born in 1921 in Bucks County, Pennsylvania, under the name Mary Ann Boyer. She later married Captain David "Bull" Conklin, a whaling sea captain, in 1851 and traveled with him to the Puget Sound. Rumor has it that Mary Ann was stubborn and may have nagged her husband a time or two—or three. After one such disagreement, the sea captain left Mary Ann stranded in Port Townsend, Washington, a small settlement just fifty miles northwest of Seattle. Without a backward glance, Captain Conklin sailed to Alaska, devoid of his wife. Mary Ann wasn't the type of person to sit back and mope; she didn't need a whaling captain to tell her how to run her life. She refused to await his return; instead, she traveled, by herself, to Seattle. When she reached Seattle, Mary Ann got a job managing the Felker House, which was located near First and Main Streets, under the watchful eye of Captain Leonard Felker. At the time, the Felker House was run as a hotel, and it provided a place for visitors to rest their heads before venturing back out to the sea and mines. Some say that Mary Ann was drawn to Felker, as she had a special draw to ship captains. However, she was never romantically involved with Felker—or any other man, for that matter. Her focus was on her business.

Funeral procession. *Courtesy of Seattle Municipal Archives.*

Felker House. *Courtesy Seattle Public Library.*

Felker transported the prefabricated building that would become his hotel on the brig *Franklin Adams*. He purchased the land—known as Maynard's Point—from its owner, local physician David "Doc" Maynard. Historians note that Maynard was pragmatic about drinking and prostitution, as well as developing his own ethical codes; this trait later came in handy for Mary Ann. The two-story Felker House was brought to life with pulverized lumber from Yesler's Mill and southern pine floors. Unlike the crude, wooden structures that lined Seattle's streets in the mid-1800s, the Felker House was built to withstand the test of time. The Felker House was the first structure in Seattle to be constructed using finished lumber. Felker and Maynard may have conspired to open a brothel, but Mary Ann was the one who brought the dream to life. Mary Ann eventually opened Seattle's first hotel under the direction of Felker. Under Mary Ann's management, the hotel was a top-notch establishment, with clean sheets and good food for a fair price. She ran a tight ship; everything had a place, and everything was in its place.

The name Mother Damnable didn't come from her dirty business dealings; rather, it came from her foul language and fiery temper—don't forget, her husband abandoned her in a small settlement to fend for herself. She had to be tough, or she wouldn't have survived. While she was married to a sea captain, Mary Ann picked up a somewhat legendary, unrestrained skill with language that allowed her to curse in Chinese, English, French, German, Portuguese and Spanish. Her nickname later metamorphosed into Madame Damnable when she decided to diversify her hotel business by opening one of Seattle's first brothels on the upper floors of the hotel. Mary Ann wasn't the type of woman to sit back and let life happen; instead, she took charge and forged a life for herself that provided ample wealth.

Mary Ann was a proficient business operator and rented out the brothel's unused rooms during the daytime. Not every unused room, however, was rented out for entertainment purposes; one of her tenants was the territorial court, which rented a room for $25 per day—the equivalent of $750 today. The profitable brothel brought an influx of money from sailors, military men, fishermen and local businessmen. The best stories from the brothel, which detail the adventures of Madame Damnable, contain both men and yelling; both of these things seemed to be her favorites, and she was very knowledgeable of both.

During a territorial court lynching trial in 1854, a few of the rooms at the Felker House were transformed into a courtroom. The case was extensive and took a great deal of time to complete. Jim Masachie, a local Native American who was working at Yesler's Mill, was accused of murdering the wife of Luther Collins. Collins gathered two friends and publicly lynched Masachie. In retaliation, two of Masachie's friends lynched two white settlers, which sparked tensions between the natives and settlers. The grand jury was deciding on two lynching cases, and careful consideration was needed to keep the peace between all parties. A lengthy trial ensued and involved the territorial government. The charges to Felker House and Madame Damnable piled up quickly; the territorial government racked up quite a bill for food, lodging and room rental. When the trial ended, one man was elected to meet with Madame Damnable and face the final bill. As the prosecuting attorney paid the bill, he asked for a detailed receipt. In most transactions, this is a reasonable request; however, some people don't like being questioned, and this sent Madame Damnable into a rage that included hurling firewood, shouting and cursing at the defenseless attorney. As she tossed the wood, Madame Damnable yelled, "You want a receipt, do you? Well, here it is!" Historians report that no one ever asked her for a receipt after this incident.

Another story about Madame Damnable began when the U.S. Navy ship *Decatur* was anchored in Elliott Bay. The job of the sailors aboard *Decatur* was to protect settlers from the hostile Native Americans. In their efforts to safeguard Seattle, the men of the *Decatur* attempted to construct a road through town. Madame Damnable didn't like these men messing around near Felker House, and she especially didn't want them tearing down the trees and brush that cloaked the questionable establishment she was running. Since Madame Damnable wasn't one to keep quiet and sit back, she caused mayhem for the sailors. Lieutenant Thomas Phelps called her a "demon in a petticoat" and a terror to the men who were serving under him on the *Decatur*. He reported that his team would rather deal with an entire Native American army then receive one lashing from Madame Damnable's tongue. Phelps reported that every time he and his men appeared, so did the so-called demon. She had an apron filled with rocks and three dogs that were ready to tear the men limb from limb. The men retreated to their ship while curse words and stones were being hurled toward their backs—an entire group of naval men running in fear from one small woman.

It wasn't until the ship's quartermaster, Sam Silk, stepped in that the men took charge over the madam. Madame Damnable took a step back when she encountered the quartermaster, who rendered her speechless. He offered her a commonsense approach and explained the importance of the roads, but his plan changed when she nearly struck him in the head with a piece of wood. On his second attempt, he rendered her speechless. Silk launched insults at the madam in a fury and ended with, "You're a damned pretty one, ain't you." With that, Madame Damnable offered him one last dirty look before she dropped her stones and wood and retreated inside Felker House. After that encounter, the rock-hard woman left the men from the *Decatur* alone.

There are very few photographs of Madame Damnable that exist, but some photographs of the Felker House show a woman standing and peering out from the balcony; this woman is believed to be Madame Damnable. Perhaps the only concrete proof of her exists in old census records and scattered accounts from historians that list the name Mary Ann Boyer. Madame Damnable died in 1873, and her remains were laid to rest at the Seattle Cemetery, the first official municipal cemetery in the city. The cemetery was located on a parcel of land that was donated by pioneer David Denny. Denny initially gave the five acres to the city as a space for its first park, but bodies were being dug up in the surrounding area to make room new buildings—a central burial location became a necessity. John Denny, the father of Arthur and David, was laid to rest at the Seattle Cemetery in 1875.

By February 1884, a proposition was brought to the city council to move the bodies that were being held in the cemetery and convert the land into a community park, as it was initially intended to be. However, the task of

When Mary Ann Conklin's grave was moved from Seattle Cemetery to Lake View Cemetery, her body turned to stone. *Author contribution.*

relocating 232 bodies to another location was overwhelming. Part of the problem was that no one knew exactly who was buried and where they were buried. The cemetery's records were mediocre at best, as the land was provided for public use and there weren't many regulations regarding burials. The city council hired a team to track down the family members of the buried individuals. Each family owned the small lots of land in which their loved ones resided; this prevented the city from taking direct ownership of the land, even though the property was a donation from Denny to the city.

The team that was hired to track down the families was able to organize information, but they couldn't remove any of the bodies. That task was given to undertaker Oliver Shorey in July 1884. Shorey was tasked with exhuming and reinterring all of the bodies at the cemetery. He was also paid to move all of the monuments and stones that were associated with each body. His final task was to build a new cedar coffin for each body. The city made this task worth his time and trouble by paying him $3,000. While body removal was just another day of work for an undertaker, Shorey hit a stumbling block almost instantly.

By August 1884, Shorey had completed around half of the removals. He used great care to ensure that all of the bodies, and their parts, were accounted for, treated with respect and kept safe. The task was difficult, as many families had still not claimed their loved ones. There had also been a fire that destroyed multiple wooden markers, leaving many graves unmarked. Shorey took his job seriously and did not let anything prevent him from successfully relocating the cemetery. Once the identity of each body was documented, a more significant glitch arose.

The land itself proved to be one of Shorey's most significant obstacles. Washington's weather is often wet, and the area frequently flooded. So, water damage eroded the ground and ate away at the wooden coffins. With little protection from the elements, the bodies became saturated with water and mud. Nature is efficient in breaking down human corpses and wooden coffins, but the presence of water inhibits the natural process of decay. Water damage can cause the rate of decomposition to vary and sometimes even halt. Wood soaked in chemical solutions can petrify in a few days. In a dry environment that is void of sitting water, a body inside a coffin decomposes instead of becoming petrified. Usually, the only way a person can see a petrified body at a cemetery is if it jumps from behind a tombstone with an unforgettable "boo." However, the land at the Seattle Cemetery produced a few somewhat haunting discoveries.

Shorey began to note that the bodies that had sustained the most damage were waterlogged and that the accompanying coffins were quite heavy. The bodies appeared gray and hard as stone; the gray coating that covered the bodies was believed to have been a substance called grave wax or adipocere. This substance forms from the anaerobic bacterial hydrolysis of the fatty tissue in a corpse. When grave wax develops, it creates a solid, petrified cast of the body's fatty tissues and internal organs, which makes the body hard as stone.

Madame Damnable carried stones in her apron pockets to toss at people when she deemed it necessary. The rocks and her mouth were her weapons of choice, so when her body turned to stone after her death, it didn't surprise most people; but for the undertaker who removed her coffin from the ground, it was a great surprise. Her body had only been in the ground for eleven years, but when Shorey attempted to remove her coffin, he noted that it was tremendously heavy, and he required the assistance of five men to move the coffin. He estimated that the coffin weighed around four hundred pounds, which was at least twice what it should have weighed. Curiosity caused the men to open the lid of the coffin, and what they found inside rivaled the stories on which urban legends are based. Her form was full-sized and perfect; her ears, hair and fingernails were still intact. While her facial features were somewhat distorted and covered in a thin, gray dust, her body appeared to be made of white marble. Madame Damnable was able to cast one last stone, and she even made the men curse while they tried to make her move.

Madame Damnable's body was relocated to Lake View Cemetery, where it now resides. Some say that the location of her body—near the edge of the cemetery's boundaries—was due to the difficulty of moving such a heavy coffin. While Seattle legends tell the tale of a woman who was cold as stone in life and turned to stone in death, experts believe that her metamorphosis was due to nothing more than a wet environment and grave wax.

PUBLIC INTOXICATION BY BEAUTY

Lou Graham

*G*erman-born Dorothea Georgine Emile Ohben entered the world on February 9, 1857. Historians and locals identify her by her stage name, Lou Graham. The wealthy madam operated an upscale brothel to which no other facility could compare in the heart of downtown Seattle. Graham was thirty-one years old when she arrived in Seattle in 1888. She came with a small amount of money and a dream of obtaining wealth. While she was best known as a madam, historical records clearly show that she made an excellent contribution of money to the educational system and children of the area.

The late 1800s was not an easy time for women; they struggled for equality and fought to find their place in the new world. Early female settlers in Seattle didn't have the right to vote, and they certainly wouldn't be seen working in any of the male-dominated careers in the area. Changes needed to occur, but progress was long and slow.

In 1854, women earned the right to vote in Washington, but this was overturned by one vote. It wasn't until 1871, when Susan B. Anthony and Abigail Scott Duniway lead a crusade through the territories of Washington and Oregon, that women began see a cultural turn. The law that granted women the right to vote was overturned many times, and the primary reason for this could be traced back to liquor control laws. Women voters were making it increasingly difficult to sell liquor, and not everyone in the city thought that turning it dry was a good idea. So, pro-liquor lobbyists contributed money to politicians who would keep women out of the voting realm. The right for women to vote was not granted until 1910, but when it was granted, reforms ravaged the area. Liquor licenses were revoked, and brothels were closed; stringent laws strictly regulated both vices. A woman holding any dominant position was not welcome, let alone a woman who ran a brothel that attracted the business of unsavory people. Like the strong women before her, Lou Graham was not stopped by this opposition.

Historian William "Bill" Speidel described Graham as a woman who stood at about five feet two inches tall and who, at the chest level, was about three feet thick. She wore plumed hats and rode around in extravagant carriages. She was often seen traveling around town in her carriage, advertising her business and encouraging businessmen to visit. Speidel recognized Lou Graham in his book *The Sons of Profit* and stated that Graham was just as influential in the city as many of the men who helped build Seattle. Graham had the necessary training in the fields of business and prostitution to be successful. Seattle was also still lacking women, so Graham struck while the business was hot.

According to Speidel, one of the best authors of historical texts in the Pacific Northwest, Lou Graham was John Furth's silent partner from the time of her arrival in Seattle until her death in 1903. Furth provided the capital, real estate and political connections that Graham required to establish the city's leading parlor house. It was common for people to seek Furth's assistance with loans and financial backing. There were times in which he felt like an idea was sound but knew that it wouldn't pique the interest of his board of directors. In these cases, the transactions went to his silent partner, Lou Graham, who offered informal, high-interest loans. Her money was even influential in saving the Puget Sound National Bank from bankruptcy during the Panic of 1893.

Graham wasn't interested in opening a brothel that was comparable to the existing brothels in the area or even one that was better than the rest; she wanted her brothel to have the quality of an elegant hotel with comparable prices. Graham felt that a brothel didn't need to be viewed as a seedy attraction, and she didn't believe that they should remain hidden in the dark. Much like her style of dress, Graham's business was colorful and visually pleasing. Graham did business differently from other brothels in the area, which charged based on how busy they were on a given night and the services they offered; Graham posted her prices openly. The qualifications that women had to meet in order to work for Graham were also much higher than those at other brothels. She required her workers to be beautiful and intelligent; candidates who wished to work for Graham were required to be able to hold conversations on subjects like opera, politics and current world events. Graham even had several girls who were multilingual and smart enough to give her male customers a run for their money. These high demands from Graham generated higher-quality workers and a higher-quality clientele at her establishment.

Graham opened her first brothel on the corner of Third and Washington Streets. The brothel resembled the other buildings in the area, and like them, it succumbed to the Great Seattle Fire on June 6, 1889. But the fire didn't stop Graham. Like other tough and feisty women from her era, Graham rebuilt the brothel using the profits from her business, and it was bigger and better than it had been before. Although her business was less than two years old, Graham was able to construct a new stone building on a parcel of land that was much larger than her first. Graham opened her newly constructed and exceedingly sophisticated parlor house at the corner of Third and Washington Streets.

With the elaborate rebuild, upper-class businessmen had a place to discreetly have a drink, discuss politics and indulge in erotic pleasures. Graham even offered free services to all government representatives, ranging from political officials to law enforcement officers. This policy not only promoted the positive image that she was trying to display, but it also

The great fire took Lou Graham's first brothel. *Courtesy of Seattle Municipal Archives.*

A plaque from the side of Lou Graham's famous building. *Author contribution.*

helped to keep her in good standing with the most important men in town. Historians believe that more official government business was conducted at Graham's brothel than at city hall. Speidel remarked that if a businessman could not describe the interior of Graham's brothel, he was not a man to do business with and couldn't be accredited for his skills.

During this time, Seattle was young and still establishing its legal precedents. At times, prostitution was legal, but at other times, it was either frowned upon or overlooked. There were times in which Graham was required to keep her business dormant and well hidden. Thankfully, she had men on the inside who tipped her off when it was time to lie low.

In July 1889, four women and two men faced arrest after a raid on Graham's establishment. Many of the brothels in the area had closed, but Graham kept conducting her business, which frustrated those who were opposed to a brothel. Graham was one of the women arrested, but she enjoyed her freedom after paying a small fine. One of the arrested women didn't have enough money to pay for the bond, so she negotiated with the courts to leave the area instead. One of the men was given a smaller fine then Graham, but that was only because he promised to testify against her. This was the only instance in which Graham faced jail time, but that fell to the ignorance of the arresting officer, who didn't recognize her. Despite the witnesses and call for a trial, the case was short-lived when it reached the judge's hands. The judge and Graham were close friends; she nodded to the judge, who offered her a smile in return. In the end, the jury trial ended in an acquittal and the end of Mayor Henry White's political career, as he resigned after witnessing the grand injustice that was done to Graham. Graham, however, went on about her day as if nothing had transpired. In August 1889, another local house of ill repute experienced a raid. This time, Graham's place was not on the list for investigation. Graham was in good standing with many of Seattle's top political officials and law enforcement officers, which helped her avoid the pitfalls of many of her competitors.

By 1894, everyone in town had a basic understanding of the wealth that was held by Lou Graham and of the luxuries inside her home, which was sometimes referred to as White Chapel. The nickname came from the famous area in London of the same name, where Jack the Ripper committed his murders. Some Seattleites believed that the name was fitting for a house of sin. Regardless of her home's name, Graham's name was well known, and her manner of dress was well appointed. She always left the house in large, overelaborate hats, fancy dresses and luxurious jewels.

In February 1884, police arrested two men for stealing two gold watches; Jim Burns and Ed Page had been carrying out robberies all over town.

A postcard titled "The Sewing Circle" features a gathering of Lou Graham and her girls. *Courtesy of Seattle Public Library.*

Luckily, they were stopped before they could set their plan of going after Seattle's most exquisite madam into action. This heist would have entered the history books as the most daring and profitable in Seattle history. While questioning the men, detectives received a clear view of the danger that Graham had been facing. The men had made their way into the Washington Street brothel to scope the place out and learn where Graham kept her diamonds. They wanted one necklace; everything else would be a bonus. The piece in question featured twenty-one diamonds—the largest of which weighed over three carats—and each stone was graded at the highest level. From the moment Graham purchased the diamond necklace, it was the talk of the town due its cost and the great brilliance of its stones. The approximate value of the necklace was well over $4,500. It would have been difficult to sell, as it was one of a kind, but the men had a plan. It would be harder to trace if it was deconstructed, and the design made it easy to break apart in order to sell the diamonds individually. Graham also wore solitaire diamond earrings, which were valued at over $700, and in her hair, she wore a miniature dagger that was accented with diamonds. The additional jewelry added another $250 to her net diamond value. But this was not all the jewelry that Graham owned; she also had four bracelets that were covered with diamonds and estimated to be worth nearly $1,000 each.

The robbers merely planned to knock on Graham's front door and seize her when she answered. They figured that they could overpower her and strip her of her diamonds quickly and efficiently. They then planned to abscond with the jewels and meet at a predetermined location. What these newcomers didn't know, however, was that Lou Graham was a remarkable woman of nerve and had defended herself numerous times. More than once, she threatened to protect herself in any manner that was required. It's entirely possible that she would have given them the fight of their lives, and the girls working for her would have retaliated as well.

Excitement returned to Graham's establishment in 1890. Graham was known for bringing in abandoned and neglected women whom she felt she could train. These women, who had been mistreated by their husbands and found themselves on the streets for various reasons, held a special place in Graham's heart. Due to her friendly nature, Graham often took in runaways and homeless women. On one occasion, her kind heart placed her between a female boarder and a jealous ex-boyfriend—not everyone left the incident alive. The newspaper headline read, "A Victim of a Siren."

Months before the fateful night, a Canadian man named John Anderson was working as a clerk in his father's hotel in Victoria, Canada. Anderson was from an affluent family, and his father didn't approve of the attention his son was showing to a young woman by the name of Elva Marsten. She was not the pure, innocent woman whom John's father intended him to court. John's father threatened to disinherit him if he pursued any relations with the young woman. When Anderson confronted his father with a gun and an intent to harm, his father requested that he be arrested. John was advised to leave town and never return under threat of spending time in prison. He chose to flee town and follow Marsten to Seattle, but little did he know that she had been taken into Lou Graham's brothel.

When John discovered this information, he turned his back on Marsten and didn't look back. Marsten followed a distraught Anderson back to room seventeen at the Auzera House, where he had reserved a room for himself. He allowed Marsten into his room, and the two conversed briefly. The young woman explained that she and Anderson could no longer be together, and just after she shut the door, a shot rang through the halls. The shot was followed by scream, and commotion filled the hall, waking most of the guests at the Auzera House. When John was found by police just moments later, the young man was bleeding profusely from his abdomen, and he was unconscious. He was moved to his bed before the doctor arrived and attempted to stop the bleeding. Shortly after the doctor's arrival, Anderson regained consciousness long enough to tell officials that he wanted to visit with his mother. A telegraph was sent from Seattle, but it was uncertain whether he would survive the night. It was said that he suffered very little, as he was typically unconscious, but during his waking moments, he called out for his beloved Elza Marsten. But she was not present, as friends had taken her to Graham's place, distraught and confused. Officials declined to bring her to Anderson, because they were afraid of what a visit from her might have done to the dying man's condition. He grew weaker by the moment and died before the evening hours. His mother did not arrive before his passing.

In 1903, Graham was in San Francisco, California, when she succumbed to syphilis, a sexually transmitted disease caused by bacterium *treponema pallidum*. This disease is difficult to diagnose during its early presentation. In the early 1900s, doctors also did not have enough information to treat such a diagnosis properly; thus, it was often deadly. Graham's remaining family members were still in Germany, and initially, the administrator of her estate was an employee at the Puget Sound National Bank. After a long process, her estate funds were given back to the City of Seattle and, eventually, the King County schools.

AGGRAVATED ASSAULT
ACT ONE

John Considine

*O*n September 29, 1868, an American impresario and pioneer of vaudeville was born in Chicago, Illinois. John Considine grew up attending Catholic school, and before he left the Windy City, he briefly worked as a law enforcement officer. The following was the first famous event in history that Considine experienced; he was only twenty then, but this experience solidified his mark in history books for many years.

On May 1, 1886, the workers at the McCormick plant decided to strike. This plant was responsible for creating the McCormick Reaper, a piece of farming equipment that required employees to have sixty-hour work weeks. The goals of the strike were to drop the duration of shifts to eight hours a day and to form the foundation of today's labor laws. The labor strike at the McCormick plant set a precedent for many future May Day rallies. On May Day 1886, over thirty-five thousand workers walked off the job. During the following days, tens of thousands more workers joined the strike. As the strikers' numbers grew, so did their list of demands. Strikers began asking for ten hours of pay for eight hours of work. During the strikers' first clash with police, John Considine participated in the attacks against the angry workers. On May 3, police fired on the strikers, killing at least two. Anarchists called for a protest meeting and demanded revenge against law enforcement.

On May 4, 1886, a large crowd gathered at Haymarket Square in Chicago, Illinois. Mayor Carter Harrison instructed the police not to disturb the meeting; however, the atmosphere changed when one speaker urged those around him to "throttle" the law. At that point, 176 officers

John Considine became known as the pioneer of vaudeville. *Courtesy of Wikipedia Creative Commons.*

marched toward the meeting and ordered the crowd to disperse. One radical in the crowd threw a dynamite bomb at the police, killing 1 officer instantly. The Haymarket Riots were officially underway. Police drew guns and fired wildly into the crowd of protesters. By the end of the riot, 60 officers were injured and 8 were dead. May 4 has remained as a memorial for all of those who fight for fair labor laws and the many protests that have taken place all over the United States since this fateful day in Chicago. Considine did survive this experience, but he promptly decided that it was time to make some changes in his life.

Leaving behind his brief career in law enforcement, Considine moved to Seattle in 1889, where he found a new life path. For the most part, he remained on the right side of the law by abstaining from vices, but this isn't to say that he didn't operate a business that allowed vice. He also became the pioneer of theater impresarios, the boss of a small gambling empire, a victorious business competitor to Wyatt Earp and a murderer during a drugstore shootout.

Just two years after moving to the Pacific Northwest, Considine found himself managing the first theater in Seattle. The People's Theater was a box house near Pioneer Square; Considine dealt cards there, but he never gambled. He also made a small fortune off the sale of alcohol but never drank. In the late nineteenth century and early twentieth century, western North American theater owners combined low-class theater with the business of a brothel and called this new establishment a box house. Box houses were the predecessors of American vaudeville. They featured a mix of specialty acts, including burlesque, comedy, dance and music. They also offered sexual entertainment for an additional charge, although liquor sales still contributed a considerable portion of the incomes for such establishments. Women employees would walk around while the show was taking place; they wore short skirts and blouses that dipped as far down as their waists. These women would circulate offstage, soliciting drink orders from the patrons. For each drink they sold, the women received a metal tag, which they could redeem for cash. According to historian Murray Morgan, "If the girls wish[ed] to peddle more personal wares, the management did not object." The People's Theater did well and prospered for many years.

Over time, Considine found himself mentioned in the local newspaper. Sometimes, his business was featured; other times, newspapers would print interviews in which he detailed his latest shows. At times, the press discussed one of the vices that took place in Considine's theater, which he worked hard to hide. Brawls often took place at the theater after patrons had consumed too much alcohol. These fights were often featured in the news and elicited negative feedback from the public.

One such newspaper article highlighted an instance in which Considine played referee to two women in the saloon area. Considine had been training an up-and-coming actress by the name of Lillian Masterson; he'd envisioned her playing the lead in a top attraction for his variety show. However, one of his aging stars, Kitty Goodwin, did not agree with his decision. The two ladies were arguing when Masterson struck Goodwin over the head with a beer glass. Surprisingly, the two abruptly stopped the fight and went their separate ways. Later that evening, the argument resumed when Goodwin violently slapped Masterson in the cheek; kicking and hair-pulling ensured. Considine and another man separated the two fulminating women, but the brief period of peace lasted for only ten minutes. Considine stepped in again to stop the fight; this time, Masterson had pulled a knife and cut Goodwin at least three times. She also caught Considine's sleeve, cutting him arm. After thirteen stitches and an arrest, the violence finally stopped. Considine met with Goodwin to see if he could help the two women reach a peaceful settlement. Only Considine and Goodwin ever knew what was said, but after the conference, Goodwin refused to bring charges against Masterson, who walked free. This was the first time that Considine's good name was tarnished by violence, but it was certainly not the last.

By 1894, the city council had declared that box houses were nuisances and set out to close their doors. Shutting the box houses down was easy. One of the main elements that was needed to run a box house successfully was alcohol, so the city council passed an ordinance that forbade the sale of alcohol in theaters. The city's liquor inspector personally visited every box house and spoke to the proprietors, advising them to discontinue the sale of alcohol. The following night, the police sergeant made rounds to prove that the new ordinance stood strong. Considine was an intelligent businessman, and he knew that the theater would not survive without the sale of alcohol or gambling. He knew that it was time for him to move, so he packed his bags and moved east to Spokane with the hope of opening a box house that could sell alcohol.

In Considine's absence, other men tried to run the People's Theater but failed. Profiting without liquor sales was impossible. The gold rush changed this situation, as thousands of unattached men flocked to Seattle in the hopes of striking it rich. While these men waited for proper transportation to Alaska, they needed entertainment and were eager to spend their money. The box houses were reopened and sold alcohol with the blessing of the city council. Among the first to reopen was the People's Theater, which was then under the ownership of Mose Goldsmith.

When Considine returned to Seattle in 1897, he was determined to reopen a box house and worked to regain ownership of the People's Theater. After all, it was his hard work and solid foundation that brought fortune to the theater. He knew that the theater's current owner was residing in California and that the current managers most likely worked under a verbal contract. Considine departed for California to meet with Goldsmith. In February 1898, for only $250, Considine signed a one-year lease for the People's Theater. Of course, the current renters were unhappy with this transaction.

It didn't take long for Considine to once again dominate the box house business. He brought in the finest entertainment, including one of the most famous variety performers of the time: Little Egypt. Her dancing was said to have been suggestive, and her clothing apparently barely covered her body. Some locals did not approve, but the male population flooded into the theater to sneak a peek. Now a wealthy and well-known man around town, Considine made friends quickly. Having friends in high places was beneficial for the box house owner. Considine's friend list included political leaders and local law enforcement officers. He

The Orpheum, one of John Considine's theaters. *Courtesy of Seattle Public Library.*

eventually met a young man by the name of William Meredith in 1889; the pair instantly become friends, but their connections would not gain fame until 1901.

William Meredith came to Seattle from Washington, D.C., after he was asked to obtain information about the amount of real estate the government had reclaimed from Doc Maynard. Upon completing this task, Meredith remained in Seattle and accepted a job working for the U.S. Customs Service. He eventually quit that position and went to the work for the Seattle Police Department as a detective. Soon afterward, William Meredith met John Considine. Historians state that Meredith traveled with Considine to Spokane, but the reason for his trip remains unknown. After this journey, the two men parted ways; little is known about the incident that triggered the parting of these two men. Meredith returned to his work with the police department, and Considine returned to managing the People's Theater. Their relationship continued to cool over the years, and by 1900, they became known enemies.

The Orpheum. *Courtesy of Seattle Public Library.*

The actual breakup of their friendship came in 1899, when Meredith arrested a pickpocket who was friends with Considine. The enemies, who barely acknowledged the existence of each other, finally came to a clash. At the time, the laws regarding the women who served alcohol at box houses had not changed; overall, the police were cracking down on illegal activities and arresting those who allowed their female employees to engage in gambling, drinking and special services. As with any other vice in Seattle, slipping a few dollars to the correct law enforcement officer could keep those involved out of trouble. During this time, however, Meredith was the chief of police, and the primary area of his crackdown was Considine's block.

During the hearings, Considine stated that Meredith had sent one of his cronies to collect $500 from the People's Theater as protection money. Failure to pay wasn't worth the risk, so Considine paid the man and watched him walk away. The man then walked directly to Meredith and handed him the money, and Considine watched as the money went straight into Meredith's pocket. This information all came to light during the city's trial of Police

Chief Meredith's "open city" policies, which allowed illegal activities to take place in town as long as he received a fair share of the profits. Meredith retaliated against his former friend and publicly announced during the trials that John Considine had impregnated a seventeen-year-old contortionist named Mamie Jenkins. He added to the slander by saying that Considine had also paid for an illegal abortion; although the reports are vague, most say that Mamie ruptured herself during a performance. Most agreed that Considine was innocent due to his reputable nature. This unbalance of trust turned more eyes toward the actions of the city's police chief. Mayor Thomas Humes sent word to Meredith that his resignation would be accepted; he couldn't have the police chief creating such ruckus in town.

After the trials, Meredith sent one of his officers to purchase a sawed-off shotgun that he had seen in a secondhand store. The officer obliged, as he did not know what was to occur. Feeling that he had no other choice, Meredith drafted a brief letter of resignation from his position as Seattle's chief of police. On June 25, 1901, Considine went to his attorney's office to discuss the newspaper article and statement from Meredith regarding Mamie Jenkins. He wanted a full redaction of the article and a public apology from Meredith, but his attorney could not make this guarantee. As Considine left the office, he remarked that he would sue Meredith for civil and criminal libel, regardless of his chances for a positive outcome. However, while Considine was consulting his attorney about the next steps he should take, Meredith was gathering weapons and forming a wicked plan. Meredith had already publicly announced his revenge.

Considine was later greeted by friends on the street, and they asked him if he owned a gun. Considine replied that he did not. Several men, including law enforcement officers, warned Considine to watch out for Meredith, but these rumors did little to shake Considine. He later met with his brother Tom before deciding to go home for the evening. As he left the People's Theater, Considine put a .38-caliber revolver in his gun pocket.

As Meredith walked down the street, he inquired about John Considine's whereabouts but got no answer. He made many threats, including, "This town isn't big enough to hold us both." Meredith then headed toward Yesler Way, where the Considine brothers regularly caught a streetcar. The brothers were not there, but Meredith did speak to Considine's attorney for several minutes. John and Tom normally would have been there, but they had been invited to have a drink with a good friend. Tom agreed, but John had been experiencing a sore throat and headed to Guy's Drugstore to get some medicine. Tom forfeited the invitation to get a drink and remained with his brother. Meredith caught the men as they crossed the street and accompanied them to the drugstore. John was greeted by a police officer, who reached out his hand and congratulated him on his success in the courtroom and in getting Meredith to resign. The men were unaware that Meredith was approaching them from behind; he stopped two feet from John, raised the sawed-off shotgun—just over Tom's shoulder—and fired at John. Fortunately, the shot missed, and Meredith's close range prevented the buckshot from scattering. These two factors saved John's life for a moment. Unharmed but stunned and confused, John stumbled backward. Meredith pushed his way past Tom and the patrolman. Too stunned to move, the men stood frozen while John continued to stumble on his rubbery legs, attempting to put distance between himself and his assailant.

Meredith fired again, and this time, a pellet hit John in the back of the neck. The rest of the blast hit the arm of an innocent bystander and sent prescription bottles flying at the pharmacist, Dr. Guy, who was working

G.O. Guy's Drugstore, the location of the final battle between Considine and Meredith. *Courtesy of Seattle Public Library.*

G.O. Guy's Pharmacy had multiple locations, which are known today as Bartell Drugs. *Courtesy of Seattle Digital Archives.*

in the back of the drugstore. Meredith dropped his shotgun and reached for the revolver at his hip. John, who was trapped behind the drugstore counter, called out to his brother Tom. This distracted Meredith long enough for John to charge forward and attack him; since he outweighed Meredith by more than fifty pounds, John was able to push him toward the front of the store. At this point, Tom finally snapped out of his daze and charged toward Meredith. He pulled the revolver from Meredith's hand and repeatedly struck him in the head. Although he only intended to knock his opponent unconscious, Tom fractured Meredith's skull in two places.

It was at this point that the sheriff and a deputy barged through the door and demanded that Tom hand over the gun. John pulled away from Meredith, which caused the injured ex-chief of police to slump over the counter. Tom then grabbed the gun from the deputy and forced the large crowd of people surrounding them to step back. Meredith pulled himself to a standing position, where he swayed back and forth as he scrambled to find his spare weapon. Before he could locate it, John broke free of the man who was holding him, pulled the .38 caliber revolver from his pocket and stepped toward Meredith. From three feet away, John fired at

John Considine's magnificent tombstone. *Author contribution.*

Meredith, striking him in his left side. John fired a second shot; this time, the bullet went straight through Meredith's heart. Meredith's final word was simple: "Oh." John fired a third shot, and Meredith fell to the floor, dead. The sheriff placed John under arrest. The entire incident lasted for only ninety seconds, from the first shot to the last.

Five months later, Meredith was in the ground, and John Considine was charged with premeditated murder in the first degree. Though Meredith was remembered as a crooked officer, officials were not hesitant in charging Considine with firing the shot that killed Meredith. During the trial, every second of the fight was dissected and inspected under a microscope. The prosecutor's office tried to say that Meredith received the first shot and that his shots were in self-defense; they even brought in witnesses who said that they heard six shots fired, rather than five. However, during cross-examination, this was found to be false. The prosecution also tried to claim Meredith was no longer able to harm anyone after taking several hits to the head from Tom Considine. The defense team argued that Meredith fired the first two shots and that Tom and John both acted in self-defense. They agreed that Meredith and John both fired shots, and they agreed that Tom struck Meredith with the gun and caused his skull to fracture. However, they also stated that the swiftness of the situation made it impossible for either man to have had the appropriate time to think through their actions—they acted on a survival instinct alone.

Even the Chicago labor riots came into play when the prosecution accused Considine of firing one of the fatal shots on that fateful day. The accusation angered Considine, and he retaliated by stating, very clearly, that he had never fired a gun toward a man or even faced a charge for assault until this incident. Finally, it was Meredith's own words that sealed the case. He had verbally killed John Considine a number of times when he said, "This town isn't big enough for both of us," and, "If he gets me out of my job, I'll kill the son-of-a-bitch."

On that November day, Meredith's widow, Mrs. John Considine, their children, Tom Considine and John's father were sitting in the courtroom. It was 2:30 p.m. when the jury went into deliberation; only three hours later, the members of the jury took their seats and passed their verdict to the bailiff. The bailiff passed it to the judge, who quickly inspected it before handing it to the court clerk. The verdict was read: "Not guilty."

BRIBING AN OFFICER

Police Chief Charles Wappenstein

*W*hat makes a good cop turn to unscrupulous behavior? A brief look into the history of Seattle's police department can reveal multiple reasons for which an otherwise ethical officer might accept a bribe or allow certain illicit activities to take place in the city.

Denny and his party came to Seattle in 1851, when the West was notoriously wild and untamed. As the population in the small, newly founded city grew, the need for law enforcement grew as well. John Jordan arrived in Seattle around 1860, and he gained employment as a stonemason. Working alongside the Mercer brothers, Jordan helped build the first University of Washington campus. In 1869, Seattle government officials created the position of town marshal; the marshal was meant to act as the chief of police and was allowed to make hiring decisions for the department. The person in this position was hired to keep the peace in the city and to put criminals behind bars. At the time, a marshal's term lasted for one year. The Seattle Police Department was not formed until Jordan's election as town marshal in 1869. Jordan later served as a city council member in 1870 and was elected mayor of Seattle in 1871. The problem with the slow growth of Seattle's police force was that vigilante justice was on the rise; the public wasn't willing to wait for the limited number of officers to respond to crime. Public lynching occurred frequently.

On one late evening in January 1882, an event took place that sparked talks for enhancing Seattle's police force. Early in the evening, a businessman by the name of George Reynolds was returning home from work when he was held up at gunpoint. Reynolds reached for his gun in order to defend himself, but he received a fatal shot from his attackers, James Sullivan and William Howard. Over two hundred men gathered and turned the men over to authorities just four hours after the attack. The judge let the two men go, believing that they were not likely to leave town. However, this was unacceptable to the vigilantes who had taken the men into custody; they captured Sullivan and Howard and took them to a scaffolding of boards that had been placed between two trees to create gallows. The men were publicly hanged before a crowd of onlookers, and their bodies were strung up until springtime as a reminder to anyone who thought that they could get away with robbery or murder.

Not long after the public lynching, another man was about to be set free from a Seattle prison. Police had arrested Benjamin Payne and named him a suspect in the killing of a police officer named David Sires on October 13, 1881. Payne's public intoxication had encouraged a barkeeper to kick him out of a saloon, so Sires attempted to arrest him. Sires obtained fatal injuries when Payne opened fire with his revolver. Sires was able to identify his murderer before his death. When the news of Payne's release spread,

Lynching in Seattle in 1882. *Courtesy of Seattle Public Library.*

over five hundred men gathered to capture him, and the bells in town were tolled three times to let Payne know that he would be the third to die. The wall of the jail was torn down, and the crowd was able to access Payne's jail cell. During the raid, Sheriff Louis Wyckoff suffered a fatal heart attack. The mob dragged Payne to the makeshift gallows where the bodies of the other two men remained. Payne protested his innocence, but his pleas went unheard as the crowd roared. Officer David Sires went down in the history books as the first Seattle police officer to lose his life in the line of duty. Seattle officials did not press charges against the vigilantes, but they did put a plan in motion to build their police force.

By 1896, the Seattle police force only had forty-three officers to maintain law and order for over six thousand people. These officers were limited even further, as they were required to patrol in forces of five or six officers for safety reasons. The small size of the police force substantially limited the area that it could cover during each shift. The officers were paid very little and were expected to work seven days a week while living in small dormitories; needless to say, law enforcement was not a popular career choice. With these unfortunate circumstances, it's easy to see why an officer in Seattle at this time may have been encouraged to participate in graft in order to fill his pockets with a little extra padding. Giving into vice offered fringe benefits, an item the force was sorely lacking.

Charles "Wappy" Wappenstein was working his way to the top of the police department in Cincinnati, Ohio, in the late 1880s. He zipped through the ranks and made detective in record time; he eventually took on the role of chief of detectives for the department. Cincinnati was a corrupt city in the late 1800s, so Wappy was able to receive his street cop training early. He quickly learned that life was rough on the meager salary of a police officer, but with the right skills, anyone could fill his pockets with extra cash from the seedier areas of town. Police officers were able to line their pockets with bribes as they looked away from certain crimes. They even helped political officials accomplish their given tasks. However, Wappy learned another lesson when he was removed from the commission on June 7, 1885; crime doesn't always pay. Once his public image was tarnished, it was time for Wappy to leave town.

Wappy left Ohio and headed west. He landed in Portland, Oregon, where he worked as a private detective for a private agency called Pinkerton National Detective Agency, which was founded by Allan Pinkerton in 1850. Today, the agency still offers services that range from private security to private military contracting work. It is the largest private law enforcement agency in the world, and Wappy entered its service when the company was still young.

In Portland, Wappy met Minnie Benn, who was the daughter of Samuel Benn, the founder of Aberdeen, Washington. In 1891, Wappy and Minnie were married, and eight years later, they celebrated the birth of their son, William. Their daughter, Joan, was born the following year. With the troubles of his departure from Cincinnati behind him, Wappy was able to form the perfect life with his beautiful family and decent job. However, his tainted image proved, once again, to be unfortunate.

The Wappenstein family arrived in Seattle around 1900. There, Wappy

Charles Wappenstein was known for his sharp appearance. *Courtesy of Seattle Public Library.*

gained employment with the Seattle Police Department. Historians describe Wappy as barely standing five feet tall; he always sported a full mustache, had a noticeable wart on his left cheek and was frequently seen wearing a pinstriped suit and a derby hat. Historian Murray Morgan described him as "soft-spoken" and "exuding considerable warmth." Public officials, fellow law officers and citizens eagerly accepted this pleasant newcomer. The vice scene in Seattle wasn't much different from that of Cincinnati at the time. Miners, fishermen, settlers and local businessmen grew bored and needed venues where they could spend money. Brothels, bars and gambling dens opened their doors and gladly accepted the money that was poured into them. City officials and law enforcement officers found it easier to look away from the smaller crimes that didn't appear to harm the public. In Seattle, the term "open city" came to life. Eventually, the allowance of criminal activity provided income for the city. There were many attempts to overthrow those who supported the open city, but those who were in favor remained firmly in charge.

At the helm in 1908 was one of Seattle's most shameless mayors, Hiram Gill. Born in Watertown, Wisconsin, on August 23, 1866, Hiram Charles Gill moved to Seattle in 1889. Seeking employment, he started waiting tables at a waterfront restaurant in the city. He later left his mark as one of the city's most controversial leaders. In 1900, voters elected Hiram to the Seattle City Council, where he served for three years as the president and slowly made a name for himself. Under the watchful eyes of Mayor Tom Humes, Gill learned everything he needed to know about running an open city.

Meanwhile, Police Chief William Meredith sought qualified officers to work Skid Row's beat. Skid Row held the most vice and highest crime rates in town. Among the most promising of Meredith's officers was none other than Charles Wappenstein. Wappy was a competent and virtuous officer; he learned quickly and knew which areas of town required the most observation. The International District, which Wappy frequently worked, thrived on underground gambling clubs.

Seattle mayor Hiram Gill. *Courtesy of Seattle Municipal Archives.*

Many of the owners of these gambling clubs bribed officers in order to gain their protection. Some of these gambling houses even had secret doors and passages, where customers could hide from the public and police. Wappy and his partner investigated the underground clubs and found their way inside, where they began collecting money from the owners. They then pocketed a share and gave the rest to Meredith.

Meredith went to war with John Considine and needed his top officers by his side. Meredith and Considine were once friends and business partners, but Considine grew angry when Wappy arrested his pickpocket friend. Wappy was Meredith's number one man on the street, and he had captured many of Considine's friends for various reasons. The battle between the pair ended with Meredith's resignation and his eventual death at the hands of Considine. While Wappy was not directly involved in the trials or the murder, Mayor Humes took them as an opportunity to fire him.

After his departure from the Seattle police force, Wappy sought alternative employment. There were some in the area who knew he was a great detective and investigator. His police skills far exceeded the standard, so he was never questioned. He eventually gained employment as an investigator with the Great Northern Railway. During this time, he grew close to the company's vice-president, J.D. Farrell. Farrell had backed Judge William Hickman Moore's race for mayor of Seattle, so after Moore's appointment, Farrell called in a favor. He asked that Wappy be appointed to the position of chief of police. At the time, the chief of police could serve for only one year before he was replaced. While Wappy later said that this was the dullest time in his entire career, the public in Seattle felt that his was perhaps one of the most influential police administrations in the history of the city.

Wappy also found employment with the Alaska–Yukon–Pacific Exposition, where he was appointed the chief of security forces. Some would argue that, when he accepted the job, Wappy's real intent was to steal funds from the company, but when the exposition closed, the president of the company reported, "Wappy did a first-rate job." He was declared a hero when he and his men located several underground tunnels through which people were sneaking into the area and costing the company over one hundred dollars a day.

When Mayor Moore lost his second election, Hiram Gill took over the office and left his mark. Gill's first action as mayor was to reinstate Police Chief Charles Wappenstein. Gill saw no problem with an "open city" and felt if the vice stuck to Skid Row, he had no problem with those who violated the city's liquor, prostitution and gambling restrictions. The public was not surprised when Wappy stepped into action and called a meeting with all of the brothel and gambling club owners. He proposed a straightforward plan of operation to these owners: they would pay the police ten dollars per month, per girl, to keep everyone involved out of jail and under the radar of the police. The thing that Wappy liked as much as police work was control. He eventually controlled the entire area called Skid Row and all of the businesses within the district. Handling the riffraff on Skid Row was a task that even William Meredith knew Wappy could handle. New and old brothels, gambling clubs and box houses were able to open their doors, but they presented one issue to Mayor Gill: they weren't staying within their designated area. Instead, they spread throughout the city, and the public was not pleased. Seattleites knew that Wappy and Gill were the two behind the city's influx of vice. The area that was once named Skid Row—or the Tenderloin—was temporarily called Wappyville.

It took a preacher named Dr. Mark Mathews to take down the dynamic duo. First, Mathews demanded Gill remove Wappy from his position as chief of police, but Gill refused. Though little was said publicly, when Gill neared his reelection, he needed the preacher to be silenced. Some believe that Wappy sent his men to threaten Mathews, but whatever the case, Mathews kept his mouth shut and was always seen carrying a pistol.

In 1911, Mayor Gill lost the election to George Dilling. Most of Gill's votes were from women in the area who had just received the right to vote and possibly worked in the fields that were protected by Gill. However, not all women voters worked in an illegal industry; the first woman to vote in Seattle was Rebecca Hall, an eighty-year-old who cast her vote for Mayor Gill.

One of Dilling's first actions as mayor was to fire Wappy. He then tried to revise the wrongdoings of the Gill administration, and both Hiram Gill and Charles Wappenstein were investigated for their actions. Some were surprised to see Colonel Alden Blethen, the publisher of the *Seattle Times*, testify at their trial. Blethen was a known supporter of both Gill and Wappy; he publicly titivated their actions in the daily newspaper. His testimony pleased Wappy, and an officer played personal bodyguard to the newspaperman.

Finally, Hiram Gill was no longer serving as mayor. He moved on as if nothing had occurred and attempted to run for office again. Charles Wappenstein, on the other hand, took the fall. He went to the state penitentiary in Walla Walla, Washington, where he was sentenced to serve time for three to ten years. Wappy was officially charged with graft in July 1911, when two men testified to bribing the police chief with $1,000. While Gill was eventually reelected and served for a total of three terms as Seattle mayor, poor Wappy found himself confined by the walls of the state

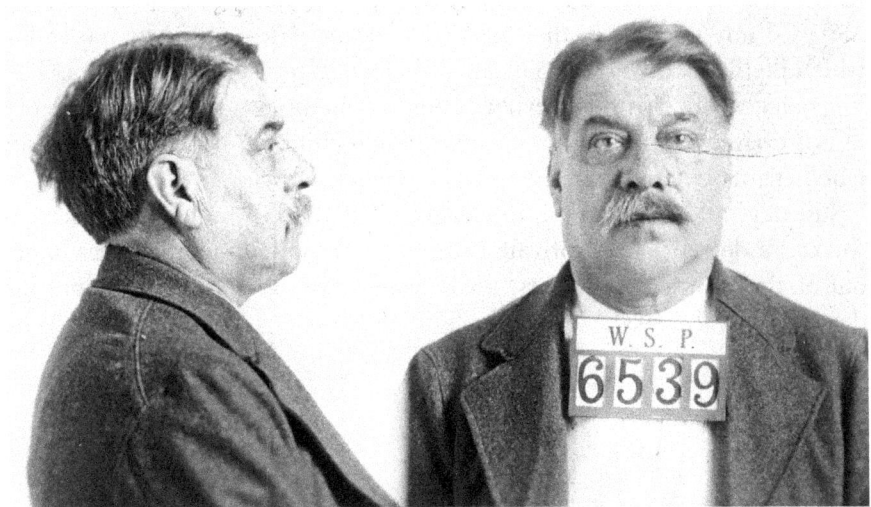

Charles Wappenstein's mug shot. *Courtesy of Washington State Penitentiary.*

The graves of Charles Wappenstein and his wife, Minnie. *Author contribution.*

penitentiary. While serving time and taking the heat for the crooked Mayor Gill, Wappy applied for a governor's pardon.

In May 1913, a reporter met with Wappy and stated that he was a different man from the one who had entered the penitentiary. Instead of a pinstriped suit and fancy hat, Wappy wore suspenders, a hickory shirt and a straw hat, which were all marked with his prisoner number: 6539. From then on, the only thing he ever investigated was whether the farm chickens had laid any eggs or if they needed tending. The same newspaper for which Blethen worked, the *Seattle Star*, helped Wappy gain his pardon. The journalist pleaded with Governor Lister to remember Charles Wappenstein as a husband and father of two exceptional children, not as a policeman who became entangled in the webs of politics and vice.

Just days after his pardon, in December 1913, Wappy had job offers to work as a detective for a private firm. Charles Wappenstein kept his name out of the Seattle newspapers, apart from a few brief mentions, until his death on July 27, 1931.

IMPERSONATING A DOCTOR

Dr. Linda Hazzard

Those who frequently travel to the Seattle area know where to stop for a nice, warm bowl of clam chowder and a basket of fish and chips: Ivar's, one of the best-known seafood and chowder houses in the Pacific Northwest. Scandinavian immigrants and Seattle pioneers Johan Ivar Haglund and Daisy Hansen Haglund gave birth to Ivar Johan Haglund on March 21, 1905. In 1938, Ivar Haglund opened his first aquarium in Seattle next to Pier 54. Haglund learned how to run an aquarium from his visiting cousins, Greta and George Smith, who ran their own aquarium in Seaside, Oregon. Haglund was a brilliant businessman, and he knew that the Great Depression was hard on everyone. He wanted to entertain and feed the public, and he tried to make a positive change in a dark and wicked world. As a young boy, Haglund learned how to play the guitar and sing folk songs, so he sat on a stool in front of the aquarium and did just that. He entertained the crowds of waiting people with songs about the critters that were held inside the aquarium. People flocked to the waterfront to wait in a notoriously long line and pay a nickel to be entertained with great folk music and the creatures Haglund collected.

In 1938, soon after the aquarium opened, Roy Buckley opened a fish and chips counter. The restaurant was located next door to the aquarium, which was filled with fish. Haglund was quick to strike a deal with Buckley, and their little enterprise quickly became a success. A local restaurant named Steve's eventually closed its doors after claiming that the small fish and chip stand put it out of business. The competition only encouraged Haglund to build a

Above: Ivar's first restaurant at the Port of Seattle. *Courtesy of Seattle Municipal Archives.*

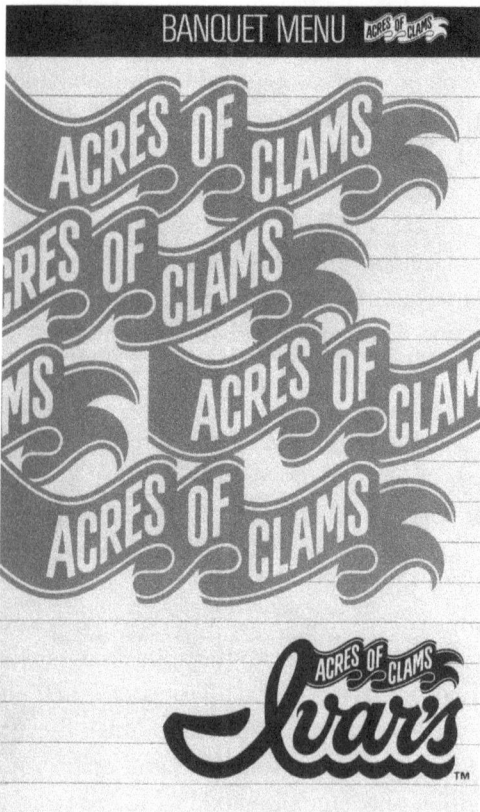

Left: This menu proves that Ivar was eager to feed locals and visitors the great temptations of the ocean. *Courtesy of Seattle Public Library.*

bigger and better counter. Less than ten years later, Haglund expanded his fish and chip counter to fine dining and opened a full restaurant on Pier 54 called Ivar's Acres of Clams. Perhaps it was Haglund's excellent sense of humor that allowed a fish and chips counter next door to an aquarium to be successful, or perhaps it was just his desire to both feed and entertain the people of Seattle.

Pat, the seal, was perhaps one of Haglund's most important staff members; Pat even accompanied Haglund on one of his most notorious publicity stunts. Haglund dressed Pat in a pinafore and lace baby cap and took him to a local department store to get a photo with Santa. Haglund arrived at the store pushing Pat in a wicker stroller. One time, Haglund even tried to match his prize octopus, Oscar. Haglund wanted to host a wrestling match between Two-Ton Tony Galento, who was an over-the-hill prizefighter, and the octopus. The stunt generated a ton of publicity, but, sadly, Oscar passed away before any real human-to-octopus match could take place.

Haglund liked to be funny and make people laugh. When his neighbors along the pier posted signs discouraging people from feeding the seagulls, Haglund responded with a sign that encouraged the opposite. He said, "I don't want to embarrass my neighbors. They do what they want to on their pier, and I'll do what I want to on mine. I consider seagulls the unpaid guardians of public health. They keep the waterfront free of garbage. They are beautiful, useful scavengers." Today, visitors to the fish and chips counter can still feed the seagulls their leftover french fries. Once again, Haglund offered food to those in need, but this time, the ones in need were animals. Haglund had a great compassion for all living creatures, and he had a need to nourish them.

Haglund is one of the most prominently known restaurateurs from Seattle. It may seem strange to discuss one of the city's top restaurateurs in a chapter about starvation, but there is a good reason for it. Ivar Haglund chose a career that provided thousands of individuals with delicious seafood, and his food became so popular that visitors to the area added it to their bucket lists. He even encouraged people to feed the seagulls along the pier and provided meals to both humans and animals. However, his mother, Daisy Haglund, was one of the first people to die while attempting Dr. Linda Hazzard's starvation cure.

Linda Burfield was born on December 19, 1867, in Carver County, Minnesota. Some credit Linda with being a feminist and a strong leader for women in her time. She was trained as an osteopathic nurse, which meant that she was prepared to practice osteopathic, or alternative, medicine.

Linda was also an author. When she combined these two talents, Linda was able to promote her experimental cure. She believed that fasting was the cure for all diseases and physical ailments. Linda experimented on people who were willing to seek out her knowledge and advice. Her treatments involved serving patients meager portions of vegetable broth and forcing them to endure long and painful enemas and forceful massages. Linda believed that these treatments allowed her patients' digestive systems to rest and be cleansed and that this would clear the body of impure blood and diseases.

At the time, Linda was not alone in believing these theories. Fasting was a common practice and was written about in medical journals and books by renowned scientists and doctors. Linda added her personal touches, like enemas that went on for hours and involved up to twelve quarts of water and deep massages that caused her patients to cry in pain. During these massages, she would shout, "Eliminate! Eliminate!"

Mrs. E. S. Extreme bilious symptoms with stupor and nausea. Fast of twenty-two days while pregnant with child whose picture is also shown. Photograph taken six months after birth of child.

A page from Dr. Linda Hazzard's book, *Fasting for the Cure of the Disease. Author, Dr. Linda Hazzard.*

Her first treatment-related death occurred in Minnesota. The coroner determined that the cause of the patient's death was starvation, and he sought legal action against Linda. But Linda found her first loophole; she wasn't a doctor and, therefore, wasn't licensed to practice medicine. Since she did not have a license, Linda couldn't face a malpractice lawsuit. At the time, this loophole allowed her to go free, even though the coroner also noted that the patient's valuables had gone missing. Linda's patients were willing victims who sought medical care from an unlicensed professional.

A few years later, Linda met and married Samuel Hazzard. They were not able to celebrate as much as they would have liked; after all, Samuel was busy facing bigamy charges since he neglected to divorce his first wife—he would have rather served two years in prison for his crime. The couple found a new life in Washington, where Linda found another loophole that allowed her to practice medicine under the title of "doctor." Despite her lack of a medical degree, the State of Washington had grandfathered in some practitioners of alternative medicine, including Linda.

Just forty miles outside of Seattle, the Hazzards found a home in Olalla. Linda warmly called the area "Wilderness Heights." She yearned to build a sanitarium in which to practice her fasting cure, but she needed money. In 1908, Linda wrote her first book, titled *Fasting for the Cure of Disease*, which detailed her advanced fasting treatment and promised readers a cure for any disease, including cancer. The sale of her book made enough money for Linda and Samuel to begin constructing several cabins, which would be used to house Linda's patients undergoing treatment, on their property.

In 1908, Daisy Haglund went to Hazzard for treatment after reading advertisements that detailed a cure for her stomach cancer. With her husband's blessing, Daisy sought treatment from Hazzard. Daisy was placed on a fast and died fifty days later. She was thirty-eight years old and left her husband and three-year-old son behind. Daisy's death certificate listed that her official cause of death was stomach cancer. Johan Haglund believed that the treatment was working and that his wife had passed from stomach cancer. He even supported Hazzard's treatment throughout the court hearings, which came much later.

Linda's first few victims fell into virtual silence. Patients died, and the Hazzard family grew richer, as they were able to trick people into signing over their belongings upon their deaths. Dr. Hazzard also signed many of her patients' death certificates, which meant that she could record any cause of death. She never chose starvation. In her practice's later years, Hazzard teamed up with Butterworth Mortuary in Seattle. Rumor has it that she paid off the mortuary to hide her patients' bodies in caskets with other bodies.

Working closely with the mortuary created the perfect situation in which Linda could scam wealthy people and hide the evidence. In local author Gregg Olsen's book *Starvation Heights*, he highlighted the tale of the Williamson sisters. Dorothea "Dora" and Claire Williamson were victims-turned-saviors in the story of Dr. Hazzard. The sisters came from a wealthy European family and were staying in Canada when they heard about Hazzard's practice. The sisters sought new and exciting ways to spend their days, and they both had small medical ailments that might have benefitted from this unique treatment. They were also Hazzard's favorite type of patient: young—in their early thirties—and wealthy. The sisters also often traveled and wouldn't be missed by family and friends until it was too late. When the sisters left for Dr. Hazzard's practice, they neglected to tell their family where they were going, as they were afraid that they would be criticized by their conventional family about the unorthodox treatment.

In 1911, the year the sisters started their treatment, five more victims died while in Dr. Hazzard's care. These statistics weren't made clear to Dr. Hazzard's potential patients or to the public. Dora and Claire began their treatments while living in an apartment in downtown Seattle; the apartment was furnished by Dr. Hazzard, who made medical visits to their home since the cabins in Olalla weren't quite ready. As days of treatments passed, the sisters grew thinner and weaker. Neighbors began to question their deterioration.

Just two months after the sisters started treatment, Dr. Hazzard knew that she would need to move them to the cabins and her home as soon as possible. At this point, the sisters were so emaciated and delirious that they required medical transport to travel. Before their departure, Dr. Hazzard jumped onto the opportunity of having the girls meet with her attorney. With a shaky hand, Claire was able to sign the documents and give Dr. Hazzard around thirty-two dollars per year for their treatments. An additional line on their medical paperwork noted their wishes if they should die while under Dr. Hazzard's care. If they died, their bodies were to be cremated and disposed of under the direction and supervision of Dr. Hazzard.

When the sisters arrived in Olalla, the cabins still weren't complete, so the Hazzards moved the sisters into their private home. With the sisters comfortably moved to Olalla, Dr. Hazzard continued to decrease their diet and administer the torturous enemas and massages that played a part in her treatment. As the sisters grew weaker, they both considered stopping treatment, but as each day passed, the doctor reminded them that they would feel better once the process was completed. Eventually, Dora and Claire were separated; Claire was quickly growing weaker and had to be kept in the house, while Dora was moved into one of the completed cabins.

Later that same month, the sisters' childhood nanny, Margaret Conway, received a somewhat cryptic telegram from Dora. She was visiting family in Australia at the time but set sail straightaway to check on the girls. Samuel Hazzard met with Margaret at Dr. Hazzard's Seattle office. At this time, Margaret was told that Claire had passed away and that Dora had gone insane. Margaret asked for proof of Claire's passing, so Samuel took her to Butterworth and Sons Mortuary to show her an embalmed body. While the body didn't resemble Claire, Margaret believed Samuel's story, including the part in which he said the embalming process had changed Claire's appearance.

After the pair left the mortuary, Samuel took Margaret to visit with Dora. When they arrived, Dora was sitting alone in her cabin, which Margaret described as a "shack." Dora was nothing more than skin and bones. She weighed around fifty pounds and couldn't even sit down without pain radiating through her body. The moment she saw Margaret, Dora begged for her to take her away and stop the treatment. However, Dora soon changed her mind and remained set on accepting all of Dr. Hazzard's treatments.

Margaret stayed with Dora in her cabin for several days, sneaking her food. The time quickly passed, and Margaret was still with Dorothea in July. Hazzard's patients all gathered for a July Fourth celebration, which was uncommon at the sanitarium. At least two patients used the celebration as an opportunity to approach Margaret and beg her to take them away.

One day, Margaret observed Dr. Hazzard wearing one of Clair's silk dressing gowns and hats. Margaret questioned the whereabouts of Dora and Claire's belongings. Hazzard explained that Dora had signed her power of attorney over to the Hazzards, which allowed them to help themselves to the sisters' funds and belongings. Margaret was furious and demanded to leave with Dora. Sadly, this did not happen. Dora had been coerced to sign over legal guardianship to the Hazzards when she fell ill. Hazzard informed Margaret that Dora would remain in their care until she died, but Margaret refused to give up hope.

Margaret summoned another relative, John Herbert, to Washington for assistance. John was a lawyer and was able to negotiate with the Hazzards. They presented him with the Williamson sisters' bill, which had reached over $2,000. Hazzard instructed the relative that Dora could leave once their debts were paid. After tense negotiations, Herbert talked Hazzard down to a sum of $1,000 to remove Dora from her property and treatment, but all of Dora's belongings had already been claimed by Hazzard.

Once Dora was safe, Herbert took the matter to the local authorities and supplied them with enough evidence to launch an investigation. Investigators found numerous cases of suspicious deaths and curious financial transactions. After the investigation, authorities had enough evidence to charge Dr. Linda Hazzard with the first-degree murder of Claire Williamson. During the trial, Dora, John and Margaret all testified against Dr. Linda Hazzard. Many of the victims' family members, however, came forward and sided with Hazzard. Daisy Haglund's husband remained a strong supporter of Hazzard, despite the death of his wife. Lawyers tried to prove that Hazzard had starved her patients until they died, stole their valuables and tricked them into signing over their money, assets and power of attorney. Hazzard's

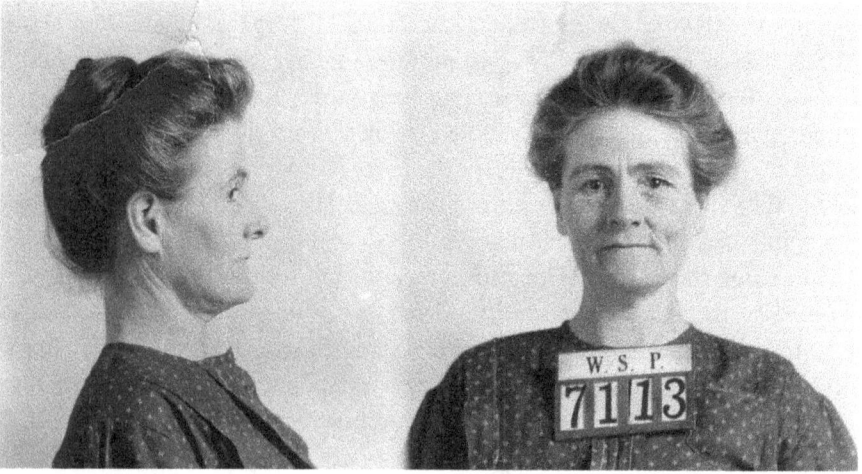

Dr. Linda Hazzard's mug shot. *Courtesy of Washington State Penitentiary.*

legal team fought back, stating that each victim had come willingly to seek Hazzard's treatment, and they claimed that other medical professionals approved her treatments. Hazzard claimed that anyone who had died under her watch had died from the original diagnosis that had brought them to her.

The trial also discussed the possibility that Dr. Hazzard had dissected her victims' bodies in her bathtub for easier disposal and that she had worked with Butterworth's Mortuary to exchange bodies for viewing by relatives. Some believed that her victims were laid in the coffins of other clients to lower the cost of the burials and to keep them discreet. Dr. Linda Hazzard defended herself by saying that she was a health practitioner who practiced unorthodox methods, but the jury didn't agree. They stripped her of her medical credentials and found her guilty of manslaughter. Her original sentence was two to twenty years of hard labor. Linda ultimately served two years at Walla Walla State Penitentiary.

After her release, the governor offered her a pardon if she agreed to leave the United States. She did so for a short time before returning to Washington. After her return, she built the sanitarium that she had dreamed of years prior, and she reopened her doors for business. Again, patients came and went. Most died as victims of Hazzard's treatments.

Finally, in 1938, Linda fell ill herself. Believing the best treatment was fasting, she began treating herself with the same "cures" she had given to at least fifteen patients in the past. Hazzard did not fare better than her patients, and on June 24, 1938, Dr. Linda Hazzard died from starvation.

CONSPIRACY TO SMUGGLE ALCOHOL

Officer Roy Olmstead

*B*y the late 1800s, people felt a lot of trepidation when it came to alcohol. Who, if anyone, should control, manufacture, import, possess and consume alcoholic intoxicants? Should social issues, such as race, religion, education and gender, play a role in the regulation of alcohol?

Before the arrival of saloons, fur trappers traded alcohol to Native Americans for fur pelts. Even at that point, the British government had restricted the amount of alcohol that was allowable for trade. The goal was to eventually eliminate all trade of liquor with the Native Americans. British officials believed that offering alcohol to Native Americans would cause them to become intoxicated and disruptive, which, in turn, could lead to a retaliation against their reign.

The Hudson Bay Company dominated Washington for many years, and it was able to survive with the occasional partial trade of alcohol for goods. However, as more American ships began to travel down the West Coast, the Hudson Bay Company found itself competing with other traders. After all, rival traders could enter the area and trade with the Native Americans, who had taken a liking to spirits. Because of this, trade between the Native Americans and the Hudson Bay Company was diminished. By 1831, however, the British had forbidden the trade of alcohol between the Native Americans and the Hudson Bay Company. Luckily, the company's chief factor, John McLoughlin, found a loophole. His company would sell alcohol to other traders, who would then "give" it to the Native Americans as a gift—there were no laws that forbade giving alcohol as a gift.

Over the next few years, the national government made several attempts to regulate alcohol, and Washington was no different from the rest of the United States. Washington voters initially turned down Prohibition; at this time, saloons played an essential role in society. They provided a central location for loggers, fishermen, fur trappers, miners, gamblers and even lawmen to gather and socialize over a cold drink. While they offered a space for social interactions, many saloons also provided entertainment. This entertainment would come in the form of dancers, billiards, darts, games of chance and, sometimes, prostitution. Alcohol was an essential component of saloon society, and many opposed any regulation of alcohol. However, like anything else, there were always those who didn't care for the vices that surrounded saloons and the consumption of alcohol. The construction of railroads and the development of new brewing technologies made the distribution of alcohol much easier, and concerns began to grow over the need for regulation. By 1909, 30 percent of voters were leaning toward a "dry" environment. With this high rate of concern, regulations needed to be put in place. The new restrictions hit saloon owners, and soon, women and children were no longer permitted to enter a saloon.

On November 3, 1914, Washington voters approved a measure that prohibited the manufacture and sale of alcohol statewide. However, this

Prohibition led to the dumping of alcohol. *Courtesy of the Library of Congress.*

measure did not affect the consumption of alcohol. Some believe that this law was passed because women had been given the right to vote in 1910, but whatever the case, all saloons were ordered to close their doors on or before December 31, 1915. Individuals with special permits could purchase alcohol out of state and import up to two quarts of hard alcohol or twelve quarts of beer every twenty days. Individuals could also obtain a prescription for liquor, which could be filled by local drugstores. The ability to obtain a prescription for liquor significantly increased the popularity of local drugstores and created the opportunity for more pharmacies to open throughout the state.

The National Prohibition Act was in place from 1920 to 1933. Washington adopted a statewide prohibition in 1916, four years before the national act. While Washington residents long supported temperance, there were outliers who refused to allow the state or the government to stop them from purchasing, selling and enjoying a drink. Because of this demand, bootleggers sprung to life. Bootlegging is the act of making, transporting and selling an illegal item without following restrictions or paying taxes, and it is most notably associated with alcohol.

Roy Olmstead was born on September 18, 1886, in Beaver City, Nebraska, to farmers John and Sarah Olmstead. He moved to Seattle in 1904, at just eighteen years old, and he worked briefly at the shipyard until he was hired by the Seattle Police Department on May 16, 1907. Olmstead was known as an outstanding officer and quickly rose through the ranks in his department. Just three years after joining his department, Olmstead became a sergeant. This promotion made Olmstead one of the youngest police sergeants in Seattle Police Department's history. Olmstead's brothers, Frank and Ralph, also joined the police department. Due to his brilliant performance, Olmstead was promoted to acting lieutenant in 1917, and he was officially promoted to lieutenant on January 22, 1919.

While Olmstead went down in the history books as being a successful police officer, he wasn't always on the right side of the law. His popularity came from his descent into the world of bootlegging. After earning the title of King of the Puget Sound bootleggers, Olmstead was perhaps one of the most notorious bootleggers in the Pacific Northwest, and his name became known worldwide.

With new laws and the regulation of alcohol, Seattle police conducted raids and arrested those who were unwilling to follow the new guidelines. Along with his fellow officers, Olmstead participated in several raids and arrested a great number of bootleggers and rumrunners. He knew the

Early Seattle Police Department badge. *Author contribution.*

bootlegging business inside and out, as one has to think like a criminal to catch a criminal. Olmstead knew the laws and how to avoid run-ins with law enforcement. His law enforcement experience eventually gave him the edge against his competitors.

Olmstead was first arrested on March 22, 1920. Nine men were captured by federal agents, including Lieutenant Olmstead and Sergeant Tom Clark, who were both highly regarded within the police force. Olmstead was working his way toward the Meadowdale dock to meet his next shipment when he was spotted driving around a roadblock that was set by the Bureau of Prohibition. Olmstead was meant to pick up a delivery of ninety-six cases of liquor—most likely rum—that were valued at well over $14,000. Instead, his clandestine bootlegging operation came under the eyes of Prohibition officials. The federal agents definitely had knowledge of a large shipment of liquor that was entering the port at the Meadowdale dock, and they knew that a band of bootleggers was bringing the shipment in from Canada. A laborer by the name of John Auth was booked and taken into police headquarters for safekeeping. He had made a statement that indicated he was stopped and questioned by Clark, who had flashed his police badge, while driving his truck. The federal agents then knew that at least one police officer was involved in the importation of illegal liquor. Olmstead and Clark easily put down $5,000 for bail and were released. Both men were dismissed from the police force while they awaited trial. They both claimed a demurrer and stated that they were unjustly arrested, as the federal agents didn't have the appropriate evidence to prove that they had taken part in the delivery of the liquor. Their final fine was a mere $500.

While his career in law enforcement was over, Olmstead wasn't disappointed. A legitimate job in the police force only made a meager income, while bootlegging allowed him to live in luxury. Olmstead saw his dismissal from the force as an opportunity to place all of his attention on bootlegging.

The following year, Olmstead's wife made the news after her car slid into a ditch on icy roads. His wife reported that she was driving down the road when her vehicle slid into the ditch. Her vehicle also struck three men who were working on a concrete mixer; when she hit them, the men were pinned between the trench and the mixer. She was arrested but was later released without any formal charges. One of the three men did not survive the accident.

Olmstead's moral standards made him a fair and honest businessman, even if he was working illegally. At the time, many bootleggers watered down and added chemicals to the alcohol they carried in order to help double their supplies. Olmstead, however, did not; instead, he imported his alcohol from Canada and sold pure, high-quality liquor. He also didn't partake in other vices, such as prostitution, narcotic sales, gambling and selling weapons illegally. He only imported alcohol from outside the Prohibition-struck United States and sold it for a profit. Many didn't regard Olmstead as a criminal; he took care of his workers and was a well-respected boss. Olmstead didn't allow any of his workers to carry guns, but he encouraged them to prioritize their safety. He believed that their lives were more important than the shipments of alcohol.

By 1922, people began accusing Roy Olmstead of being the ringleader of the biggest rum smuggling ring in the Pacific Northwest. He was arrested again but was released on $1,000 bail. This time, agents recovered over $20,000 worth of liquor from the home of Eddie Gay, one of Olmstead's men. By the time of his second marriage, in 1924, Olmstead's bootlegging business was doing quite well. Elise started a radio station that went under the call sign KFQX. Sometimes, her show was aired from Smith Tower and other contemporary studios, but at other times, it was aired directly from the

Olmstead home. The station's programming ranged from children's bedtime stories to entertainment features. While her program appeared innocent to listeners, some believe Elise sent out coded messages to Olmstead and his workers in her stories. She ran the radio show until November 17, 1924.

That same day, the Olmstead home was raided during her broadcast, and government agents pulled her show off the air for good. Olmstead's biggest problem was that his former co-workers knew him and knew of his bootlegging business, which made it very difficult for him to remain hidden for long. Police placed a wiretap on Olmstead's phone, and the evidence collected from it was sent to the U.S. Supreme Court for review and consideration of charges. Olmstead was a man of the law before he was a bootlegger—he knew his rights. He challenged the charges against him and argued that the use of the wiretaps as evidence violated his rights. The courts found that the evidence obtained via a secret telephone wiretap violated Roy Olmstead's Fourth and Fifth Amendment rights. The Fourth Amendment to the Bill of Rights prohibits unreasonable search and seizure and states that a warrant must be signed by a judge who has determined that there is probable cause for the search and seizure. The Fifth Amendment, among other things, protects individuals from being compelled to be a witness against themselves in a criminal case. Olmstead, along with seventy-two other bootleggers, was charged

Roy Olmstead's regal home in Seattle. *Author contribution.*

Roy Olmstead's residence remains occupied as of this writing. *Author contribution.*

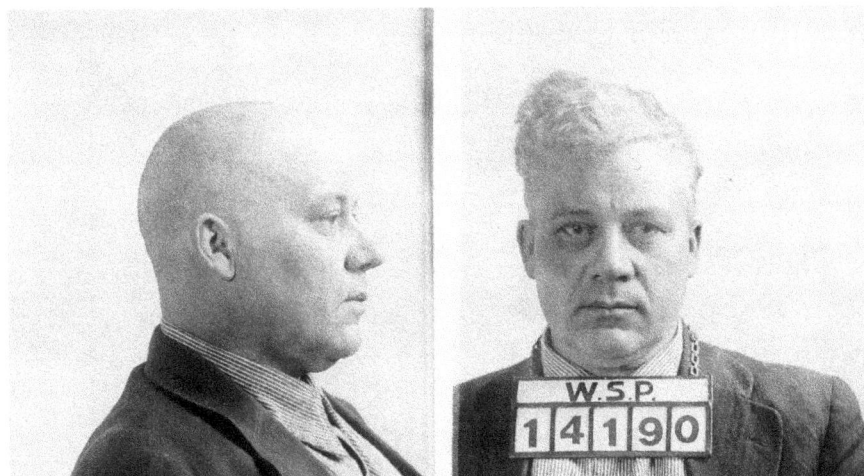

Roy Olmstead's mug shot. *Courtesy of Washington State Penitentiary.*

with conspiracy to violate the National Prohibition Act by unlawfully possessing, transporting and selling alcohol. Records indicate that those involved were making almost $200,000 per month, or around $2 million a year. As a business manager, Olmstead was netting 50 percent of all of his profits. The wiretap was not placed by trespassing; instead, federal agents placed taps near homes and locations that were known to be frequented by the men charged in the case. This evidence pointed to members of the Seattle Police Department who were helping to cover up and offer an early release to some members of Olmstead's organization in exchange for payment.

Roy Olmstead was convicted and spent four years at McNeil Island Correctional Institute. On May 12, 1931, Olmstead went home after serving his full term and an additional thirty days. He paid an $8,000 fine and was released with time off for good behavior. He was said to have been a model prisoner, which didn't surprise anyone who knew the true Olmstead. He did not return to a life of bootlegging or police work. Instead, he returned to live in Seattle with his wife and daughter. His luxurious car and home were gone, and he worked as an insecticide salesman and fumigator. On December 25, 1935, Olmstead received a full pardon from President Franklin Delano Roosevelt. The pardon restored Olmstead's constitutional rights and awarded him over $10,000. His wife eventually left him, but he continued to lead a positive life. Until his death on April 30, 1966, Roy's strong moral base overpowered his desire to return to the wicked world of bootlegging.

FAILURE TO DISCLOSE

Nellie Curtis

*D*uring the early 1900s, Seattle's population continued to diversify. Scandinavians worked in the fishing and lumber industries, African Americans worked on the railroads and took restaurant jobs and the Japanese farmed and operated hotels. The population of the International District, which is mostly home to Asian immigrants, vastly increased during this era. There were struggles; at the time, Asian Americans were the only immigrants who were ineligible to become naturalized citizens in the United States. The Chinese Exclusion Act of 1882 decreased the allowable number of immigrants from China but increased the allowable number of immigrants from Japan. By 1917, Congress had banned all Asian immigrants, with the exception of Japanese and Filipino immigrants. A few years later, Seattle began to push the Japanese out.

In 1921, the State of Washington passed an Alien Land Law, which restricted the land ownership of many Asian American immigrants. Japanese farmers filled the Seattle area in the early 1900s, and most of these immigrants planted on leased property. During the summer, immigrants often worked to harvest the region's fruits and vegetables. Some of these farmers owned their own land, but the exclusion act of 1921 prevented many from actually owning land. These individuals were forced to lease property, which created a problem for Japanese farmers and business owners. They were often kicked off of their leased land in the early 1940s, as the efforts to exclude and deport all Asian American immigrants began to kick into high gear. However, some Asian Americans in the area viewed these evictions as open doors to business opportunities. Today, Pike's Place Market, in the heart of Seattle, is known for its flying fish and attracting tourists from all over the world. However, in the 1930s, there was a different kind of attraction taking place in the market.

Nellie Curtis, who was also known as Zella Nightingale, Nellie Gray and Yetta Solomon, purchased the Camp Hotel on the corner of First Avenue and Virginia Street. By 1942, Nellie had also purchased the Outlook Hotel on the corner of First Avenue and Pike Street, in Pike Place Market. She purchased the hotels from the Kodomas, a family of Japanese immigrants who had received eviction notices for their leased properties. Curtis renamed the Outlook Hotel LaSalle Hotel and became known as one of Seattle's successful madams. The hotel, which had the slogan, "LaSalle Hotel: Friends Made Easily," offered more than just a place to sleep. The hotel provided entertainment for the local men, who still outnumbered the women in Seattle, and it serviced military men who visited the area. At times, the line at the hotel went out the door and down the road. Eventually, military personnel were banned by the government from entering the hotel and soliciting sexual acts from the women who worked there.

In 1951, Curtis sold the LaSalle to George and Sodeko Ikeda. The Ikedas recalled watching Curtis go through her drawers, searching for the keys to the front door of the hotel. Her dressers and nightstands were overflowing with cold hard cash. It was clear that she didn't have any financial concerns, but when she moved to Aberdeen, she left the new hotel owners struggling to keep the place clean and clear of its previous actions. They were able to send a few men walking in the opposite direction, but old habits die hard. Ikeda and his family went on to battle in court with Curtis.

Ikeda and his wife had worked on a farm in California before moving to Seattle in 1950 with five of their seven children. They first lived with a family member while Ikeda worked as a janitor and saved his money. In June 1951, he purchased the Strand Hotel on First Avenue. In August 1951, Nellie Curtis obtained the services of a real estate agent by the name of Frank Yamashita to sell the LaSalle Hotel. For $25,000, the buyer would receive the hotel's lease, licenses, furniture and equipment. The hotel consisted of fifty-seven rooms, and fifty-three were rentable. Ikeda was interested in making a deal. On September 15, 1951, he offered Curtis a down payment of $1,000 in earnest money and requested to pay $17,500, along with an additional $7,500 upon closing. The remaining money would be paid off in monthly payments of $200. When Yamashita reported the deal to Curtis, she declined to make a deal until she spoke to her attorney. Eventually, too

Prior to Nellie Curtis, the LaSalle Hotel was called the Outlook Hotel. *Courtesy of Seattle Municipal Archives.*

much time had passed, and the contract became void. This first contact ended with the Ikedas getting their earnest money back.

Not long after this first failed transaction, George Tucker, another real estate agent, approached Ikeda about the LaSalle Hotel. Ikeda had toured the hotel once with Yamashita and twice with Tucker. On all three visits, he was unable to meet Curtis. Workers either told Ikeda that she had been working as the night shift clerk or that she had been ill. On his last visit, he was able to speak with the day shift clerk, who stated that there were about thirty-four permanent guests and weekend guests filled the rest of the rooms. She also reported that the hotel received a few guests during the week but made no mention of any transient guests or of the brothel. Ikeda learned that the hotel's monthly income was around $2,000.

In October 1951, Ikeda again presented earnest money to Curtis and requested to buy the hotel. The battle between the pair's attorneys lasted for about ten days, but all parties finally reached an agreement for the sale of the hotel, and the Ikeda family took ownership on October 18, 1951. It was on this day that Ikeda learned there were only twelve permanent residents at the hotel. So, how did Curtis become so wealthy running the hotel? During his first day of working at the front desk, Ikeda was surprised to find that nearly twenty men had come in to ask about the girls. He was finally able to rent one room to a young man but was again surprised when the man called down to the front desk asking for a girl to be sent to his room. Ikeda explained that he didn't have any women to send, and the customer left. During the Ikedas' first weekend running the hotel, their son, Bob, came to help his father with a couple of shifts, and he found that nearly fifty men had come in asking to rent a room and a girl. Ikeda eventually posted a sign in the front window that stated, "No Girls!" It was becoming clear that Curtis was running more than a hotel. The number of male visitors and the amount of income that Curtis promised led to one likely answer: she was running a brothel, not a hotel. Ikeda sought legal action.

During the trial, evidence showed that the LaSalle Hotel was a brothel, but Curtis also had legitimate hotel guests. The hotel's reputation made it difficult for Ikeda to prove that the only income generated by the hotel originated in prostitution. Finally, Ikeda received $7,500 in compensation from Curtis, who had moved her business out of Seattle. Thankfully, as the years passed, men learned of Curtis's new brothel and left Ikeda in peace.

Curtis settled in the town of Aberdeen, Washington, just a little over one hundred miles southwest of Seattle. Aberdeen was and still is a small logging town. In the 1940s, Aberdeen drew loggers, fishermen and ship captains. Nicknamed the Hellhole of the Pacific and the Port of Missing Men, Aberdeen had a reputation of making people disappear.

In the early 1900s, William "Billy" Gohl contributed to the area's number of missing men and murders. This serial killer had a way of befriending locals who were seeking logging and shipping jobs. Men would come to town with their valuables in the hopes of finding a job. Gohl would lure the men into the bar where he worked as a bartender, and later, he would lure them in as a union official at the Sailor's Union of the Pacific. He would make sure that these newcomers felt welcome in town before he asked about their family, friends, money and valuables. Of these men, those who didn't have connections but had a suitable number of valuables often went missing without anyone batting an eye. Gohl shot and killed most of his victims in the union building before relieving them of their valuables and disposing their bodies in the river. Some historical reports suggest that a trapdoor in the union building was attached to a chute that led to the Wishkah River.

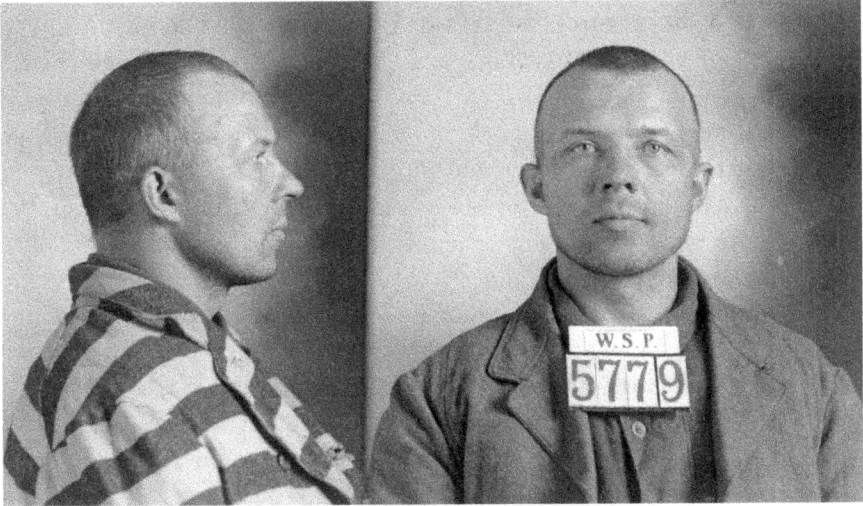

William "Billy" Gohl's mug shot. *Courtesy of Washington State Penitentiary.*

At the time of his death, Gohl, who was fifty-four years old, was standing trial for two murders, but it's believed that he killed well over one hundred immigrant men in the town of Aberdeen.

Nearly fifty years after Gohl's reign of terror, Curtis arrived in the small logging town. There, she took money from men and offered her services in return. Curtis's reputation preceded her, and it drew military men from the Tacoma area to her brothel in Aberdeen. In Aberdeen, Curtis purchased the Cass Hotel and changed its name to Curtis Hotel; here, she resumed her brothel business. She employed six girls and added five to the staff on weekends and military paydays.

Ed Lundgren became the mayor of Aberdeen in 1953. In 1958, he was up for reelection and asked the city's employees to support his bid for office; two police officers refused. Sometime after the election, the two officers were arrested at the local brothel and suspended without pay. The arrest didn't sit well with Police Chief Nicholas "Nick" Yantsin. He had long been tolerant of the town's liberal views on prostitution, but that tolerance ended after the election. Yantsin learned that brothels were political weapons. He knew that he had to bring law and order back to town, so he put his plan into action on January 31, 1959.

Reverend Lloyd Auchard, a Presbyterian minister, and Jack Mecak, a former police officer and friend of Yantsin's, assisted Yantsin by serving as witnesses. Yantsin's report later indicated that the three men were greeted at the door of the Curtis Hotel by a hefty woman at the top of stairs, who shouted, "Come on in, fellas! These are nice girls; you can hear them better with their clothes off." The woman was Nellie Curtis, and she introduced Yantsin to one of the girls, Lora Summers. Once they were in her private cubicle, Lora offered Yantsin a menu and a price list of services she provided. Yantsin took some money from his pocket, and Lora began undoing the button on his pants. Before she could proceed, Yantsin reached for his police badge and declared, "You're under arrest."

Lora shouted out for Curtis, who entered the room demanding to know what Yantsin was doing to her girl. At that point, Yantsin arrested eighteen men and women, as well as Curtis herself. The busted brothel made the front page of the newspaper and ended Yantsin's career.

Police Chief Pat Gallagher was greeted by a mob of men and women in the police station's lobby the following morning. The mayor was upset and called to ask how this had occurred. Yantsin was demoted from captain to beat cop and was forced to work the graveyard shift. A disgruntled Curtis filed charges against Yantsin, stating that he had illegally completed a search and seizure of her hotel. The case received prompt dismissal. Curtis pleaded the fifth and refused to answer any questions about her brothel and the women in her employment.

In turn, Yantsin filed charges against Curtis. This time, the judge didn't let Curtis off so easy. The court charged Curtis with running a house of ill repute and fined her $500. This brush-in with the law prompted her decision to retire. She deeded her hotel to the City of Aberdeen and fled back to Seattle, where she enjoyed the rest of her years without concern of facing a prostitution charge. However, her retirement did not go smoothly. Curtis wasn't exactly honest with the Internal Revenue Service; she cheated the government out of thousands of dollars in tax revenue during the years she ran her brothel. With accrued penalties, she owed well over $250,000. Curtis was unable to reach a settlement until 1971. She paid off $120,000 and finally found time to relax. Just five years later, at the age of seventy-five, Nellie Curtis died.

RACKETEERING
AND TAX EVASION

Francis Colacurcio Sr.

*O*ne man spent over sixty-seven years participating in corrupt activities in the Seattle area. Francis Colacurcio Sr., better known as Frank, was born in Seattle, Washington, on June 18, 1917. His family immigrated to the city from Southern Italy. Frank was the eldest of nine children and learned business ethics at an early age while working on his father's vegetable farm in Seattle. Frank dropped out of school in 1932, before completing eighth grade. He went straight into working for a produce-hauling business, and by the age of eighteen, he had opened his first business. Frank's trucking company thrived, and its success proved that he knew to succeed in the world of business.

Frank's first run-in with the law came in 1943. His first conviction came after he had sexual relations with a sixteen-year-old girl; he was twenty-five years old then and still working as a driver for his trucking company that moved produce from local farms to wholesale distributors. After his arrest, he went to the state penitentiary in Monroe, Washington, where he spent sixteen months in prison.

As his trucking company began to take off, Frank teamed up with his brother, Bill. The brothers expanded the company and began distributing vending machines, jukeboxes and cigarette machines. These were all popular items in the 1950s, and the company's profits soared. In 1957, the U.S Senate Rackets Investigating Committee subpoenaed Frank to testify in a nationwide probe on the coin-operated machine industry. The prosecutor claimed that the Colacurcio brothers were attempting to monopolize the jukebox business in Seattle. Rival operators claimed they were threatened with bodily harm if they refused to join the Colacurcio Brother's Amusement Company. No formal charges ever came to light, but the city council declined to renew the brothers' operating license. So, the pair decided that was time to expand their business ventures.

It wasn't until 1962 that Frank got involved in atrocious businesses. He held an interest in several bars, nightclubs and restaurants; he even opened the beer garden at the World's Fair in 1962. At that time, Frank introduced Seattle to topless dancing, and his title of the King of Strippers was born. In 1965, he introduced go-go dancers to Seattle at the Firelite Room in the downtown area. Just four years later, Frank racked up another charge with the law when he assaulted a bartender who was working as a police informant. By 1971, Frank's rap sheet included sexual misconduct, assault and tax evasion convictions, and he added racketeering when illegal bingo cards came to Washington. His trial exploited political and law enforcement payoffs, which helped cover his illicit gambling business and keep his activities under wraps—well, as much as a Stripper King can keep affairs under wraps. One nightclub owner claimed that he paid Frank $3,000 a month, and in exchange, Frank made sure that his club wasn't bothered by the police, competitors or troublemakers.

Frank wasn't exactly honest with the government when it came to matters of his income. The extent of his early involvement in nightclubs may never be known, but thanks to a host of associates, we know that he was a silent partner in several clubs. In 1974, he faced his first charge of tax evasion in federal court. In the early 1970s, Frank's involvement in organized crime likely increased, but his connections didn't surface until the early 2000s.

In the summer of 1975, Frank offered Everett Fretland, owner of the Wagon Wheel Restaurant and Bar in Yakima, Washington, $35,000 for his business. Frank was turned down, and an explosion and fire at the restaurant soon followed. Arson was suspected, but no arrests were made. In early September, Fretland was found dead in his bar; the cause of death was five gunshots to the back. Shortly thereafter, one of the doormen at a Colacurcio nightclub took over the management of the Wagon Wheel. No suspects faced charges, and it wasn't until 2006 that the case was reopened to investigate a possible link to Frank. The official case didn't reach a judge's ears until after Frank's death in 2010, but witnesses were able to shed some light on the subject. Investigators arrested Gary Isaacs and charged him with the first-degree murder of

Everett Fretland. The courts described the case as a contract hit disguised as a robbery. Witnesses explained that Isaacs was promised $30,000 for Fretland's death.

As Frank neared the end of his prison term in 1971, he planned to expand his strip clubs. Frank Hinkley was cited for lewd activity nearly two hundred times at his nightclubs, the Bear Cave and the Lucky Lady, and this brought fear. Frank wasn't confident that he could obtain a liquor license, and he didn't care for the publicity that Hinkley was creating. In 1974, the Lucky Lady vanished—destroyed by an arsonist. Shortly after the fire, an associate of Frank's was said to have approached Hinkley, informing him to "clean up his act." Hinkley refused to shake. Just one year later, Frank Hinkley and his fiancée, Barbara Rosenfield, were found shot to death in the Bear Cave, near Boeing Field. No arrests were made until 2006, when detectives received new information linking James Braman to the murders. Police hoped that Braman would confess a link to Frank, but he refused to talk. He told investigators, "They'll kill me." Perhaps he could have helped law enforcement, but Braman was dying of terminal liver cancer and chose to keep silent. He was released on bail only two weeks after his arrest and overdosed on methadone a few days later.

Karen Martin approached federal prosecutors in 1979 and claimed to have details on the contract killing of Leroy Grant, which occurred the previous year. Grant was found shot to death in Maple Valley, Washington, on January 26, 1978. For immunity, Martin confessed that she was offered $10,000 by an unnamed person in organized crime to kill Grant; she never received the money. She said that Grant had received the money—which he shouldn't have—and refused to return the mistaken funds. Federal investigators never turned Martin over to local law enforcement, who surely would have charged her with murder. However, in 2007, they reopened the case and formally charged Martin, who then entered a plea of not guilty and refused to cooperate.

With his stereotypical Italian flair, a keen business sense and an ability to monopolize, it wasn't long before people accused Frank of operating in organized crime in Seattle. Frank's association was strong, and the State Patrol Organized Crime Unit took note. In 1979, the Organized Crime Unit alleged that Frank controlled a crime group that was operating topless bars and clubs throughout Washington. Frank denied these charges. This was the first time that organized crime professionals investigated and poked their noses into places that were intentionally well hidden.

The 1980s kicked off a crackdown on organized crime from local and federal law enforcement agencies. In 1981, Frank fought another tax fraud charge—this time, from the money he raised at his many strip clubs. He ultimately served two and a half years in prison.

Without Frank's knowledge—or maybe he knew and didn't care—law enforcement agents met for a conference in Las Vegas. This FBI-organized event was attended by investigators from twelve of the western states, and one of their featured topics of discussion was Frank Colacurcio. In the late 1980s, authorities in Arizona indicted relatives of Frank's on alleged profit-skimming, bribery and money laundering charges. It was becoming more apparent that the Colacurcio family wasn't only dominating business in Seattle, but in cities all over the western states.

One additional murder was potentially linked to Frank. In the spring of 1985, a retired police officer was walking his dog in the woods when he discovered the skeletal remains of Rex Parsons. A large sum of cash that was found on the body ruled out robbery and pointed to murder. Parsons had a lengthy criminal history, including fraud. After an arrest in early 1984, Parsons agreed to work as a police informant for the FBI and Arizona police. His testimonies helped seal several cases that were pending in Arizona courts. For the right price, nothing was off-limits, and Frank always took a share of the profit. In the summer of 1984, Parsons flew to Seattle to obtain a construction loan. He met with James McQuade, a known associate of Frank's, at the Sorrento Hotel. McQuade was the last person seen with Rex Parsons, but he was never connected to his death. The case remains cold.

By 1991, Frank and his son, Frank Jr., were in the courtroom pleading guilty. Law enforcement officials had accused Frank of aiding in the preparation of false tax documents in 1984. Frank Jr. pleaded guilty to one charge, but prosecutors charged Frank Sr., who was also skimming profits from two topless bars in Alaska, with racketeering. A manager from one of Frank's clubs, Gilbert Paurole, disappeared into the Witness Protection Program after he testified against Frank. Frank found himself serving another two years behind bars.

In 1993, Jackie Colacurcio divorced Frank and moved to Poulsbo, Washington, to avoid the spotlight. Jackie found herself living in a modest home, with a few properties and about $3,000 a month in alimony payments. She never publicly declared much about the divorce, but it was speculated that was Jackie was tired of playing second to the girls on Frank's payroll. Two years later, Frank was again serving two years in prison for violating his probation by fondling a woman who was applying for a job at one of his clubs. During interviews for stripping positions at Frank's clubs, women were made aware of what male patrons wanted and how much they paid for sexual favors.

In 2003, Frank and his associates funneled thousands of dollars in campaign contributions to three Seattle City Council members: Judy Nicastro, Heidi Wills and Jim Compton. Frank was seeking the city council's approval to expand his parking lot at Rick's Strip Club in the Lake City neighborhood. He had already been denied twice by the previous council, so he needed the city council on his side. He had his friends, family and associates all donate to the campaign funds. Frank reimbursed everyone for the donations, which diluted the flow of money and kept his contribution undercover for some time.

In 2003, at age eighty-six, Frank Sr. was still going strong. He started the year with an assault charge that was filed by one of his waitresses. Frank was known to bring his work home with him, and the women working at his club knew that they would be paid well to entertain him in the privacy of his home. However, many of his workers wished to have no part in his sexual conquests. The dancers at all of the Colacurcio clubs were known for offering more than a pure lap dance. Some called the clubs

The sign for Rick's Night Club was not nearly as flashy as the club's interior. *Author contribution.*

whorehouses and said that they were staffed by indentured servants; this prompted an investigation into hidden prostitution charges. The dancers paid Frank "rent" for their areas each night. If they wanted to do more than break even, they needed to ensure high tips from paying customers.

In 2008, nearly sixty years after the start of Frank's ventures into the business of topless and nude clubs, the FBI agents launched a major raid of his properties. The raid included several of Frank's strip clubs, Talent West and Frank Sr.'s home. Colacurcio Sr. has long been portrayed by law enforcement and the media as one of Seattle's most notorious racketeering figures, if not its own version of the "Godfather."

With search warrants in hand, FBI and IRS agents raided four of Frank's strip clubs: Rick's, Sugar's, Honey's and Fox's. They also raided Talents West, the talent agency that was run by Frank in order to recruit strippers for his clubs. Last, but certainly not least, they raided Frank's home in Lake Forest Park. At the time of these raids, Frank was ninety years old. A temporary restraining order froze all of assets for these locations and prevented the clubs from being sold until the investigation was closed. Law enforcement officials would not close the clubs, which were generating around $5 million per month. Undercover agents, confidential informants, former dancers and pieces of surveillance technology, including court-ordered bugs, were used to obtain the evidence that was needed to encourage the federal judge to sign the required warrants.

Investigators found that while Frank's clubs fronted as strip clubs, they held a darker sin inside. The action inside revealed more than bare skin, and the women who worked there charged flat rates for sexual favors. Frank took his cut of the profit from the women and found other ways to make a profit from his dancers. The dancers paid Frank $130 per shift as rent. If they missed a scheduled shift or didn't make enough profit, they owed the club money. For many of the dancers, performing sexual acts with clients was the only way to pay this rent. Customers were able to purchase tokens from a particular machine in the club—most men didn't mind the additional $4 transaction fee at the machine—that could be used to pay the dancers for private dances. At the end of the night, the dancers would cash out their tokens, and the club manager would automatically deduct a 10 percent cut for the club.

A formal indictment of Frank Colacurcio Sr., Frank Jr., Steven Fueston and Frank's driver and associate, John Gilbert "Gil" Conte, came down in the summer of 2009. All of the men, with the exception of Conte, received charges of conspiracy to commit racketeering, conspiracy to use interstate

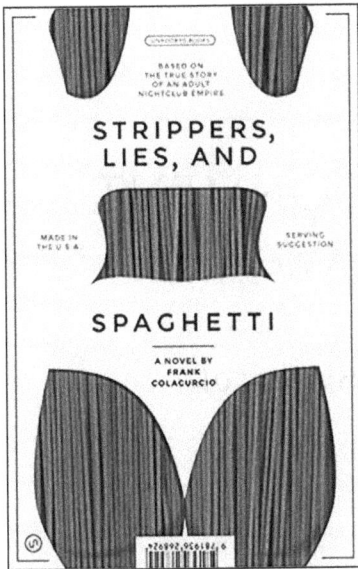

Frank Colacurcio's book, *Strippers, Lies, and Spaghetti. Courtesy of Frank Colacurcio.*

facilities in aid of racketeering and conspiracy to engage in money laundering and mail fraud. Conte received a charge of conspiracy to use interstate facilities in aid of racketeering. All of the men denied these allegations. They received probation and a ban from working in the adult entertainment industry. The government seized all of Frank's properties and closed all four strip clubs mentioned in the indictment. U.S. attorney Jeffrey Sullivan vowed to dismantle the nude dancing empire permanently. The dancers who cooperated received immunity. Sullivan stated that the charges applied to these men could carry up to a twenty-year prison sentence.

In 2010, at ninety-three years old, Frank Colacurcio Sr. died of heart failure at the University of Washington Medical Center in Seattle, Washington. His body was laid to rest at Acacia Memorial Park in Lake Forest Park. Just two months after his death, Frank Jr. pleaded guilty to racketeering and conspiracy charges; in exchange, the federal prosecutor dropped fourteen other charges against him. He went to prison for one year. Assistant U.S. attorney Todd Greenburg told the court, "This truly will be the final nail in the coffin of the Colacurcio racketeering enterprise."

WILLFUL ABANDONMENT
OF THE LAW

Prosecutor Charles Carroll

here are two Seattle men by the name of Charles Carroll, who both would fit into the theme of this book. The two men are both so deserving of being mentioned that it was difficult to keep them straight when writing this chapter. Christopher Bayley pointed this out in his book *Seattle Justice*, which details Prosecutor Carroll's takeover of the King County Prosecutor's Office, the beginning of the fall of the police payoff system and Seattle's tolerance policy toward vice. Seattle's leniency toward vice began early in the city's history, when law enforcement officers and political officials took bribes and payment in exchange for ignoring illicit activities, such as prostitution and gambling.

The economic stimulus from the Klondike Gold Rush of 1897 and World War I encouraged gambling and prostitution to expand; people had money and needed to spend it. Over the years, Seattle's mayors and law enforcement officials worked to stop these crimes, but without the full support of everyone, tolerance remained. Seattle's city council opened the doors to an open town when it passed an ordinance in 1954 that allowed card rooms to obtain licensing. This license allowed club owners to open establishments where the public could gather and play cards. Gambling was still illegal in Washington, but the city's policy of tolerance began with the card rooms. This policy of tolerance gave people a term to describe the leniency granted by the city council toward the card rooms' adherence to the state's gambling laws. Police who worked the areas populated by gambling clubs took the tolerance policy as a right to contact the shop owners and remind them that they were hosting illegal activities and were, therefore, indebted to the city. Their payment came in the way of cash bribes; the officers pocketed the money and gave a share to the city. In turn, the city continued to be tolerant toward the illicit activities. During this time, officers were able to double their income by collecting bribe money. If a club operator refused to pay, the city could suspend its liquor license until the owners were encouraged to cooperate.

It wasn't until 1967 that the depth of this tolerance policy came to light in the public. The *Seattle Times* began publishing articles that directly exposed the payoff system. Mayor James Braman enlisted a team of close friends and trusted city officials to investigate the allegations, but he was also in favor of the tolerance policy. At first glance, the team could not locate enough evidence to either confirm or deny the claims presented in the newspaper.

In 1969, attorney Stan Pitkin from Bellingham, Washington, was appointed by President Richard Nixon to investigate political corruption in Washington. The federal government lacked the authority to investigate local corruption of political and legal accounts, but local attorneys had no such restrictions. Several witnesses were called before a grand jury and questioned about the possibility of a police payoff system in Seattle. Most of

Former assistant police chief of the Seattle Police Department Milford "Buzz" Cook. *Courtesy of Seattle Municipal Archives.*

the witnesses who were brought forward for questioning were directly involved in the payoffs and didn't want to incriminate themselves. Some refused to talk and were cited for contempt, while others came in willingly and deceived the grand jury. A year later, assistant chief of police Milford "Buzz" Cook faced indictment for perjury. While under oath, Cook denied any knowledge of a payoff system or bribery taking place in the city. His perjury trial ended with his conviction and a sentence to time in prison. Then, the lid was blown off of the entire tolerance policy and payoff system.

On September 14, 1970, the task force was assigned to investigate the payoff system, which was reported to involve up to forty officers. They felt that the payoff system had officially ended in 1968 with

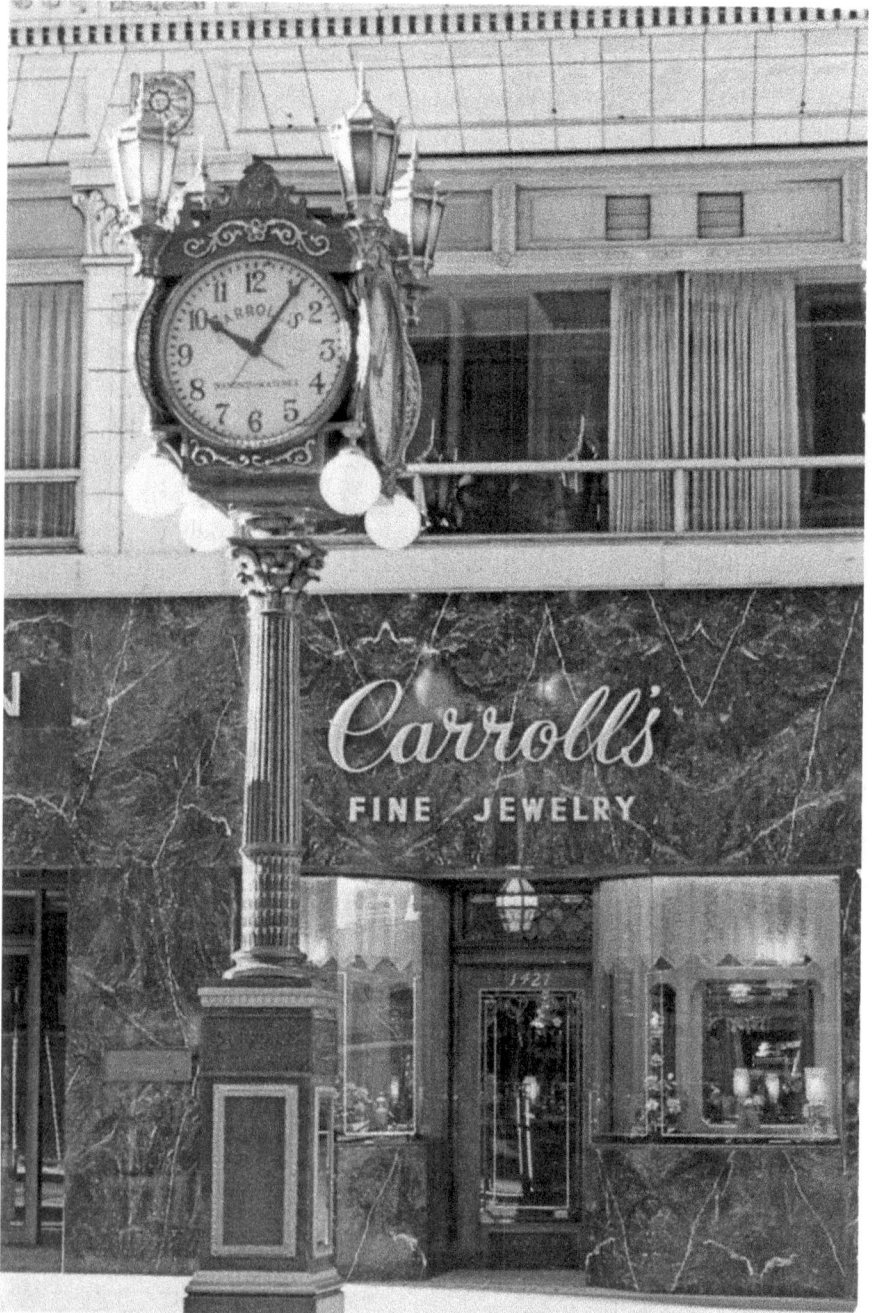

Carroll's Jewelry and its famous clock still adorn the area. *Courtesy of Seattle Public Library.*

the significant restructuring of the police department. Most of the officers who had been involved had either been dismissed, retired or quit. When the guilty officers were charged to the fullest, King County's prosecuting attorney, Charles O. "Chuck" Carroll, stepped in. He requested the charges be dropped to misdemeanors and for the officers to be suspended from duty.

Chuck Carroll was born in Seattle in 1906 to Thomas and Maude Carroll. Thomas Carroll founded Carroll's Fine Jewelry in Pioneer Square in 1895, and it was the first retailer to reside in a ten-story building in Seattle. Thomas Carroll was known for his landmark green-marble storefront, hand-painted street clock and beautiful jewels. He was also known for his generosity; just after World War II, he felt there was too much hate worldwide and gave away over three thousand gold crosses to spread good cheer. The money from the store helped Thomas and Maude provide good lives for their children.

Chuck Carroll attended Garfield High School in Seattle, where he played football. He earned sixteen varsity letters and the title of Garfield Athlete of the First Half of the Century in 1950. After his graduation from high school, Chuck went to college and played football for the University of Washington. Glenn "Pop" Warner, the founder of Pop Warner Football, College Football Hall of Fame recipient and football coach, was quoted as saying, "I don't believe there is a better halfback in the entire United States. Carroll didn't display a weakness." Chuck eventually earned his place in the College Football Hall of Fame and the National Football Foundation Hall of Fame. He was the first player to be placed in the University of Washington's Husky Hall of Fame, which earned him the right to retire his no. 2 jersey. This has happened only three times in the university's history. From 1927 to 1928, Chuck was named as an All-American running back. Despite his success, football was never Chuck's chosen career. Instead, he pursued a law degree at the University of Washington. He later graduated from law school and had a flourishing career at a legal practice in Seattle.

As an active participant in the Republican Party, he entered the army's Judge Advocate General Department (JAG Corps) at the start of World War II, and he rose to the title of colonel. Just after the war, small stakes cardrooms, bingo parlors and pinball arcades were prevalent in Seattle. Pinball arcades were able to generate over $25 million, around $200 million today, in profit in just one year. At the time, Frank Colacurcio and his men monopolized the sale of pinball machines. There wasn't an officer in Seattle who wanted to step up against the potential damages of crossing Colacurcio. If Colacurcio was happy, there would be less vice in the city. He had a way of controlling his men and other offenders in the city.

In 1948, Chuck left the JAG Corps and his private practice when he was appointed as the King County prosecuting attorney. The role of King County prosecutor had three main tasks: investigate crimes, decide whether to instigate legal proceedings and appear in court. This was a compelling position, as it had unique powers and duties that an attorney did not have. Prosecuting attorneys acted as the legal representation for the county's universal laws, including its gambling laws. Gambling money trickled upward in Seattle and made the city government very wealthy. This wealth traveled from the pockets of customers, to business owners, to the police and, finally, to Seattle's government. Brothels generated a great deal of money for the city, but the last one that existed in town was the LaSalle Hotel run by Nellie Curtis.

By 1952, the only brothel businesses in the area were located in smaller towns outside of Seattle's city limits. The only trickle-up money that was collected by the city government came from gambling. Most historians agree that Chuck wasn't monetarily corrupt, but he was hungry for power. He liked overseeing judges, police officers, attorneys and politicians. Chuck kept files on every man and woman he could to help maintain his influence. Everything was flowing smoothly with the payoff system, and although Chuck publicly denied his support of the system, he stuck around to protect it. Chuck's power became even stronger when he asked the men and women who worked for him to support his campaign at all costs. They were encouraged to donate to the campaign with the reminder that, if he left office, everything would change, and people would lose their jobs. Officers who didn't support Chuck eventually found pink slips. Those who helped Chuck found themselves climbing the corporate ladder and holding high-ranking positions.

When Christopher Bayley challenged Chuck for his position in 1970, no one thought he had a chance of winning against the mighty Chuck Carroll, but attorney Stan Pitkin stepped in with a quarterback sneak that no one expected. If Chuck didn't investigate the Seattle payoff system, the federal government threatened to step in and take the matter before a grand jury. Going after the king of the courtroom wasn't going to be an easy task. Charles M. "Streetcar Charlie" Carroll was one of the oldest city council members and was the chairman of the licensing committee; he was in favor of reforming the tolerance policy. With his help, the council voted to stop all licensing for pinball machines and cardrooms—two of the biggest money makers, struck from existence. Soon afterward, the bingo halls faced the same music. Streetcar Charlie's problem, however, was that he didn't work to stop others from allowing the tolerance policy. He was only willing to encourage the investigation of his counterpart Chuck Carroll.

In 1970, the campaigning began. Bayley knew that he needed to prove his worth against his opponent, who held a lot of power over Seattle's most influential voters. The most significant help to Bayley's campaign was the pending grand jury investigation that was being held over Chuck's head. Police corruption became headline news in all of Seattle's newspapers. Frank Colacurcio and Charles Berger were two of the first men to face indictments before the grand jury. Buzz Cook's trial came in June 1970, at the height of campaigning for the November election.

When Bayley met with Chuck Carroll to announce his interest in running for the prosecutor's job, he found himself flanked by two of his closest political companions: Bill Boeing Jr. and Victor Denny. Boeing often used his family name and notoriety to fund the candidate of his choice. He backed the Republican Party, and the candidates he supported were likely to win based on the campaign contributions generated by Boeing. Denny was a direct descendant of Seattle founder Arthur Denny. The three were an intimidating trio.

By the end of June 1970, the public's interest was piqued by the ongoing investigation. Numerous witnesses, including police officers, were called to testify. Not a single witness implemented Chuck, but his image was souring in the eyes of the community. Spectators didn't understand how a man of such intelligence knew nothing about the police payoff system. It wasn't until August that Chuck announced his intent to run for reelection. He assured the public of his innocence and of his qualifications to hold the office that he had controlled for over twenty years.

As November came and went, the county watched as the office of the prosecuting attorney changed hands; Christopher Bayley won the election. His first order of business was to clean up the past corruption so that the county could move on to bigger and better projects. The case was pressed further under the power of Bayley. By January 1971, he had begun to pursue the investigation. The police department, which had taken in large sums of bribe money, was still primarily intact. There were years of hard work ahead of the new prosecutor if he wanted to bring law and order back to Seattle. The big question on everyone's minds was how many people were involved in the payoffs, and how high up did it go? During any given time, the police department employed around forty men, but not all of its officers were guilty of graft. However, from 1960 to 1970, there were about seventy men involved in the payoff system, and most of those officers had left the department. There were also more than just police officers involved in the payoff system. Overall, those who served as the chief of police during that period took part in the system, as they failed to stop their officers from violating the laws against accepting bribe money. The establishment owners who paid the bribes were also guilty. Lastly, the councilmen and mayors who had conceived of and perpetuated the tolerance policy were also guilty. They played a significant role in the structuring and shaping of the complex payoff system.

The grand jury filed five indictments in May 1971. These indictments included those of two police officers, a sheriff's lieutenant, a liquor board inspector and a local criminal attorney. In June, there were two more indictments; this time, they were against two additional police officers. After the deliberation from these trials, eleven more citations were brought against police officers.

On July 27, 1971, the public heard a formal announcement of nineteen charges, which included those of high-ranking police officers, political leaders and Charles O. Carroll, Seattle's former prosecuting attorney. Officials chose to treat this case as a conspiracy, and therefore, only one trial was held to decide the fate of all nineteen men. The downside to this was that there were so many participants in the payoff system who all seemed to be backing and protecting one another. Judge Cole ruled that the effect of the changes in the law were so minute that the grand jury should not have investigated the case. Bayley disagreed and filed for an appeal, but the ruling from Cole set the case back a year. The situation dragged on until 1974; criminal trials and guilty pleas came as early as 1973 and 1974. The final

Chuck Carroll's gravesite.
Author contribution.

report from the investigation noted that many of those involved did not face charges, but the Seattle Police Department had taken efforts to purge itself of the violators—they had done their housekeeping.

Chuck eventually returned to private practice and retired in 1985. After his retirement, Chuck was able to enjoy time with his wife, children and grandchildren. He passed away on June 23, 2003, at the age of ninety-six.

THIRTEEN COUNTS OF FIRST-DEGREE MURDER

Willie Mak, Benjamin Ng and Tony Ng

The Northwest Railroad brought Chinese and Japanese workers to the Pacific Northwest to lay track and chisel through the area's mighty granite mountains. Once the tracks were completed, over ten thousand Chinese workers needed a place to call home. They eventually settled in downtown Seattle, in an area that has become known as Chinatown and the International District of Seattle. These new residents didn't always speak English, which restricted their ability to participate in recreational activities; they couldn't see a movie or watch television. Sports, like fishing and hunting, were only entertaining to those who had enough money to participate. Chinese lotteries became popular as early as 1890. Gambling and card games quickly gained popularity among the Asian American population, so residents began to stay near home.

In the early 1900s, gambling was an acceptable form of entertainment. Gambling clubs historically ran from 9:00 a.m. until midnight. The city not only supported gambling, but it also thrived as the clubs flourished. This is because the City of Seattle fined each poker table $30 per month, and each blackjack table paid the city around $100 per month. Eventually, however, the clubs decided that they didn't want to pay the city a portion of their profits. After all, the clubs' incomes were unpredictable; they may have done poorly one day and make $10,000 the next night. The speakeasy and gambling clubs in Seattle began to go underground and hide from the public eye and the police.

In 1909, three Scandinavian men named Nelson, Tagholm and Jensen ordered the construction of the 120-room tenement home at the Southwest corner of King Street and Seventh Avenue South. This building at the heart of the International District housed the immigrants who were coming to Seattle. Under the name Nelson-Tagholm-Jensen Tenement, the building provided single-room housing for workers. The original cost of the massive structure was a mere $50,000, but as time went on, it became priceless.

Through the years, the tenement was called Hotel Yukon, Hotel Ivy, Hudson Hotel and Hotel Louisa. In the 1920s and 1930s, the building housed the Hong Kong Chinese Society Club, a speakeasy. Some called the club the Bucket of Blood in reference to its large cups of beer. Beer and other alcoholic beverages held power during this time period; Prohibition lasted from 1915 to 1935 in Washington State. The Ubangi Club, an African American jazz bar, also operated in this space. Guitarist Jimi Hendrix's mother, Lucille Hendrix, was a waitress at this club and, at times, sang for its patrons. Rumor has it that the building may have had secret passageways and corridors that led to smaller, more inclusive clubs, where hand-chosen individuals could gamble in private. Records

The Wah Mee Club's early street signage. *Courtesy of Seattle Public Library.*

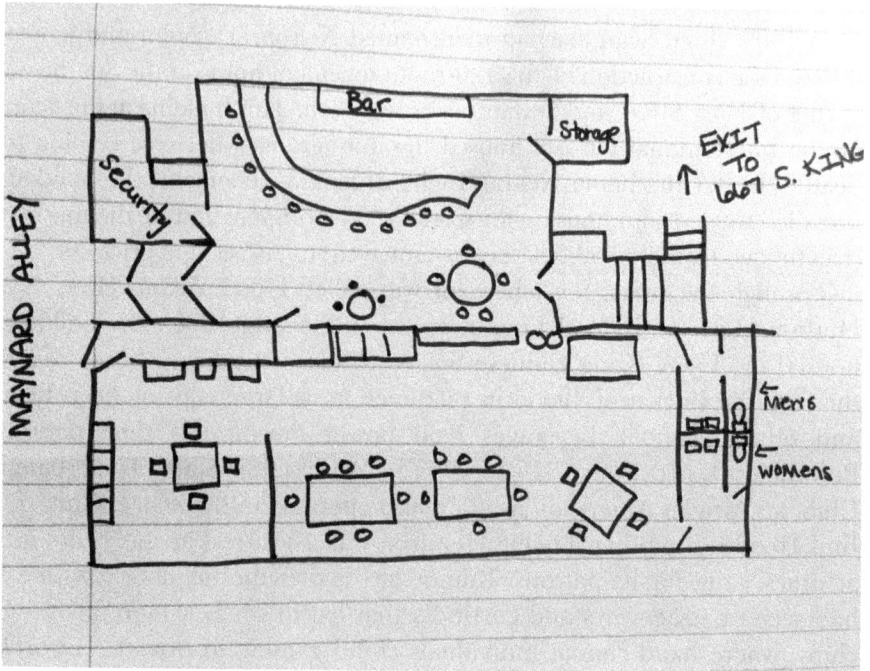

Rendering of the floor plan for the Wah Mee Club. *Author contribution.*

would undoubtedly prove that the hotel's alley led to the entrance of a Chinese social club that began operations under the name Blue Heaven in the 1920s. The club operated, hidden away in the basement of the Louisa Hotel, until the 1950s. The name was later changed to the Wah Mee, which means "beautiful China" in simplified Chinese.

The first step toward entering this exclusive, illegal club was for guests to ring a doorbell that was located in Maynard Alley. Then, a security guard would peer through the one clear glass block, which was surrounded by a series of opaque blocks. If a guest was approved, the guard would open the first set of doors, where visitors were intercepted at the first security checkpoint. Guests would then approach an additional clear glass block, where they were able to show their membership identification cards. If they were correctly identified, an armed guard would buzz the second door open, which allowed visitors to enter one of the most elegant gambling joints in Seattle. Just through the double doors and off to the left, there was a bar that curved through the room. The waiters wore black ties and served refreshments, including cigarettes, alcohol and food. The club's small storage closet was far in the back, off to the left side. It also had private doors that led to an exit through the inner workings of the building and out to South King Street. To enter the right side of the club, visitors had to go down two steps. Mah-jongg, blackjack, poker and pai gow tables filled the space. The bathrooms were hidden on the right side of the club in the very back.

Chinese businessmen and restaurant owners frequented the club in order to win big and socialize with colleagues. Those who knew the gambling scene in Seattle knew that most of the city's high-stakes gambling took place at the Wah Mee. Winners left with tens of thousands of dollars. Keeping the pockets of the beat cops lined allowed the Wah Mee Club to operate under the radar. Ownership of the building remained with the families of Nelson, Tagholm and Jensen until the Woo family purchased it in the 1970s. It continued to operate as one of Seattle's most prestigious gambling clubs until one fateful night, when the building made history for a crime of another sort.

In the late 1970s and early 1980s, illegal gambling was still in full swing in Seattle—at least in the International District. However, the early 1980s were a turning point for the Wah Mee. Most expected this elegant club to go down in the history books for its splendor, high-stakes gambling and big winners, but Kwan Fai "Willie" Mak had other plans for the club.

In 1975, Willie and his family immigrated to Seattle from the Kwang Tung Province in China. At the time, Willie was a teenager. In China, the family lived in an overcrowded apartment building. When he first arrived in Seattle, Willie spoke very little English but enrolled in high school. He worked small jobs to help his family and found profit while working as a dealer at various local gambling clubs. However, he often partook in the gambling and lost a lot of his earnings. He eventually became a petty thief and joined the Hop Sing Tong, a notorious and formidable West Coast Asian gang. He did not choose the best path to follow. By paying a twenty-dollar fee to join the Tong, Willie hoped that he could earn some extra money by dealing drugs and working at the gambling club that was run by the gang.

By the age of twenty-two, Willie was overwhelmed with gambling debt, which exceeded several thousand dollars, at one of the clubs where he worked. Willie was respected in his community, and most businesses believed that he would eventually pay his debts. However, Willie's debt kept growing, and in a few weeks, it rose from $10,000 to $30,000. Willie's frustration grew as his debt flourished. He decided that there was one sure-fire way to free himself from his obligation: he was going to rob a high-status gambling club. Willie's first obstacle was finding men who were willing to help him. He knew gang members and often hung around a seedy crowd, but most of them didn't like the stakes of Willie's plan. Willie planned to rob Seattle's most lucrative club and leave no witnesses to turn him over to authorities. Willie told his prospective accomplices that he would kill anyone who resisted him, whether he had their help or not. Choosing accomplices was difficult, but selecting a club was easy. The Wah Mee Club had both mah-jongg and pai gow tables, which drew in nearly $100,000 on any given night. It was common to see a guest at the Wah Mee wager over $50,000 at any one table; the club's clientele was made up of the International District's well-to-do and prominent community members.

Willie met with dozens of men, but it took him some time to obtain his first accomplice: twenty-two-year-old Benjamin Kin Ng. The two men had several similarities; they both emigrated from the same province of mainland China in 1975, they both belonged to the Hop Sing Tong and they both worked part-time as dealers at local gambling clubs, where they shared a passion for wagering at the pai gow tables. They had even attended the same Seattle high school. Benjamin worked part time at the Hong Kong Restaurant in the International District. He had a criminal record that was long enough to reach from one side of Washington to the next. His records proved that he had experience with guns. He was a perfect fit for Willie's plan, but Willie's debt was increasing, and he needed one more partner.

Willie held more meetings and exposed his plan to more people. He was running out of time, and if the rumors had continued to spread, he could have found himself in deep trouble. With some luck, however, Willie found his third man: Wai-Chiu Ng, better known as Tony. Though he shared the same last name as Benjamin, the two were unrelated. Tony was twenty-five years old and had a clean record. He was also born in Hong Kong but moved to the United States in 1960 with his father. The rest of his family joined them ten years later. Tony quickly earned English and helped his family with the daily operations of their restaurant, China Kitchen, in Lynnwood. Tony grew to be a quiet man who, at times, gambled but preferred to spend time at home with his girlfriend. Tony agreed to help Willie and Benjamin rob the Wah Mee Club, but he only did so because he owed Willie $1,000. Willie had promised to clear Tony's debt if he participated. While Tony agreed to the robbery, Willie's plan to silence all potential of the witnesses remained a secret. Willie needed to plan the time of the robbery very meticulously, as Seattle police officers frequented the club to receive cash kickbacks. With the details cautiously prepared, Willie set his plan into motion.

Twenty-four hours before the robbery, Tony told Willie that he wanted to back out. He borrowed money from his girlfriend and begged Willie to accept his debt. Willie refused; he needed Tony. He pulled a gun on Tony and made a definite threat. He told Tony that if he didn't help, Willie would kill his family and his girlfriend and burn down his parents' restaurant. He'd also said that he'd hunt Tony down to ensure his death.

Days before the robbery, Willie found himself at one of the International District's local gambling clubs called the Gim Lun Association, where he lost about $200,000. He borrowed $500,000 from a cook at the Hong Kong Restaurant and went on about his night. Just after 10:00 p.m., Willie headed over to the Wah Mee Club with his friend Tony. They pressed the doorbell and greeted Gim Lun Wong, who buzzed them inside. They settled around a Pai Gow table, where Wai Chin was dealing tiles. The two started with small $1 and $2 bets, but Willie had money burning a hole in his pocket, and he quickly raised the stakes. Before long, he had burned through the money he had borrowed.

On the morning of February 18, 1983, Willie met Tony and Benjamin. The three met at a Denny's restaurant in South Seattle to formalize their final plan. After breakfast, the three parted. Willie found a getaway car and went home to gather guns, nylon cords and a duffel bag. That evening, Willie, Benjamin and Tony met in the Tai Tung restaurant to share a booth and dinner. The three sat in silence, and after eating, they parted ways again. The time of the robbery was closing in quickly, and the fate of the Wah Mee looked gloomy.

That night, Willie and Tony arrived at the Wah Mee entrance together. Willie concealed his weapons from the security guard, Gim Lun Wong, who recognized the duo from the night before and buzzed them through the double entry. The two then observed the room, which held around seven or eight patrons who were all busy gambling away at the tables. The click of the tiles hitting the tables, the din of conversations and the burst of occasional laughter didn't quiet Tony's nerves. He tried to relax by sharing a plate of food with Willie and chatting with one of the dealers, Wai Chin, whom they had met the night before. Benjamin arrived around 12:30 p.m., carrying a brown paper bag filled with nylon cords. He rang the doorbell, and the guard buzzed him inside. As he entered the Wah Mee Club, he shouted, "Hands up!" And the commotion of the robbery began.

Benjamin held a gun up to the guard, forcing him to continue buzzing visitors into the club. The customers in the club were a hogtied with the nylon cords, and as new customers entered, they found themselves joining the others on the floor, tied and bound, their freedom restricted by the tight

MAR

MOO MIN   JEAN C.
1930 — 1983   1935 — 1983

人村下鄉洞會合三山台東廣

馬 馬

The gravesites of Moo Min and Jean Mar, victims of the Wah Mee massacre. *Author contribution.*

cords around their hands and ankles. Benjamin and Tony began to empty the pockets of their victims. The three men filled a bag with just over $6,000 in cash. At that point, Tony was instructed to wait in the area between the security doors and watch for anyone who might want to enter the club. Then, without notice, Willie and Benjamin fired at the thirteen victims on the floor and the security guard at the door. More than thirty rounds were shot at the fourteen victims, and not one missed.

As the victims lay still, music filled the room, and the men escaped in their borrowed car. But little did they know that one man, the dealer they'd just shared a meal with, Wai Chin, was still alive. Wai Chin was struggling to regain consciousness and wiggle himself into a standing position, but he managed to stand. He then stumbled over the victims, who were lying at his feet in pools of blood, to make his way toward the door, where he called for help. The hero Wai Chin was able to identify all three men and testify against them in court. Only six days after the Wah Mee massacre, Kwan Fai "Willie" Mak and Benjamin Kin Ng received charges of thirteen counts of aggravated first-degree murder.

In March 1983, Wai-Chiu "Tony" Ng was charged with thirteen counts of aggravated first-degree murder, even though he remained at large. In August, Benjamin was convicted of murder and sentenced to life in prison. Only two months later, Kwan Fai "Willie" Mak, known leader of the three suspects, was convicted of murder and sentenced to death. After going through a vigorous appeals process, Mak's death penalty was eventually changed to life in prison. Both men remain behind bars today.

By June 1984, Tony had made the FBI's Ten Most Wanted Fugitives list, and the Seattle Police Department reached out to the citizens in Chinatown, pleading for leads on his whereabouts. But it wasn't until October 4, 1984, that Tony found himself captured in Calgary, Alberta, Canada. Some people were surprised to hear that Tony would be acquitted of murder but convicted of thirteen counts of robbery and a single count of assault with a deadly weapon, but experts didn't believe that he was an active shooter during the massacre. After several meetings with the parole board, Tony was granted parole after serving twenty-eight of the thirty-five years he was sentenced. In 2014, Tony was released and promptly deported to China.

Wai-Chu "Tony" Ng made the FBI's Most Wanted List. *Courtesy of the Federal Bureau of Investigations.*

Tanya Woo, one of the building's owners, told an interviewer with the *Seattle Weekly*, "In respect to the families, we sealed the door after that night. Everything remains untouched, the patron's cups, jackets, the doorman's lunch." The Wah Mee Club site remained a tomb until a fire on Christmas Eve 2013 damaged the area beyond repair. In April 2015, the old section of the Louisa Hotel and its basement, which housed the Wah Mee Club, disappeared as the building turned to rubble. The Woo family hopes to build a park in this now vacated area of the building.

FEDERAL ROBBERY AND ELUDING POLICE

Hollywood Bandit

I don't want any bait bills or dye packs, got it?" This tagline is from one of the most prolific bank robbers who ever roamed the streets of Seattle, Washington. William Scott "Hollywood" Scurlock's life story reads like a mystery novel. He was a man who craved the privacy of his secluded home and the attention he earned as a model. He loved the simple, free lifestyle of the 1970s and often walked around barefoot and completely nude in his treehouse. However, he also adorned the women he dated with expensive jewels, decorated his home in rich details and indulged in only the most exceptional food and drink. Scurlock was known for his handsome appearance, intelligence and uniqueness. His friends saw him as a kind-hearted person who was willing to share his wealth when he was able. Scurlock devoted himself to whatever task was lying ahead of him, and he strived for perfection. As the years passed, a new side of this mysterious man materialized. The truth would indeed prove to be stranger than fiction when it came to the life of the Hollywood Bandit.

World-renowned true crime author Ann Rule wrote a book titled *The End of the Dream: The Golden Boy Who Never Grew Up*, which details the life of this intelligent, creative man who perhaps robbed twenty banks before his death. The book states that Scurlock "was hitting the books [at college] as hard as he would later hit the bank." Understanding Scurlock's life requires one to look back to his birth. Scurlock was born and raised in Reston, Virginia. In 1925, Andrew Carnegie's widow sold Carnegie Hall to real estate developer named Robert Simon Sr. When he passed away in 1935, his son, Robert

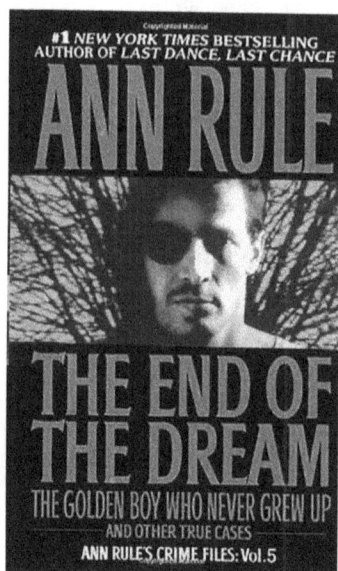

The End of the Dream by Ann Rule.
Author, Ann Rule.

Simon Jr., became the proud owner of the prestigious location. Soon after graduating from Harvard, and after taking full control of his family's real estate planning and development company, Simon sold Carnegie Hall to the City of New York for $5 million. This money funded Simon's dream of creating a planned community in Reston, Virginia, that would feature a mix of residential and commercial properties and plenty of leisure activities. He planned to surround everything with a buffer of lush, green trees in order to comfort his community's residents. His design was so well plotted that, in 2018, Reston received the honor as one of the top places to live in Virginia. Before Reston was developed, however, the area housed the Green Foresters Club, an eighty-three-acre nudist colony. This type of community wasn't unusual during the late 1960s and early 1970s. But an ominous event shaded this nudist colony and the land on which it sat.

On February 28, 1949, a murder was written into Reston's history books. Charles Holober, a member of the nudist colony, was traveling from Washington, D.C., to see the newly constructed lodge at the Green Foresters Club. He was accompanied by his pregnant wife, Frances, and their eight-month-old daughter, June. Upon leaving the lodge, it's believed that their car became stuck in the mud. A disagreement between the couple caused Frances to walk away with June in her arms and Charles to spend the night in their marooned car. In the morning, he caught a ride home, where he gathered a friend and his brother-in-law to retrieve his vehicle. Frances and June had still not returned, so the police were notified that they were missing.

An intense search left the county police, detectives and local Boy Scout volunteers at a standstill. Late in the evening, just as searchers were ready to concede, one of the detectives noted that the ground he was standing on was soft. In a shallow grave—only eighteen inches beneath the surface—near the lodge and less than two hundred feet from the Holobers' car, the police found the bodies of Frances and June. Evidence showed that Frances had

Above: Southwestern State Hospital, where Charles Holober spent time. *Courtesy of Virginia State Digital Archives.*

Left: Police located a shallow grave in Reston, Virginia, where they recovered the body of a mother embracing her baby. *Author contribution.*

been beaten before she was shot once in the head and once in the heart. June was buried alive, held in her mother's loving embrace. Charles later confessed to the murder, which he had planned three weeks earlier. The first jury sentenced him to die in the electric chair, but an appeal found him not guilty due to reasons of insanity. This overturned sentence allowed him to walk free in August 1968. Nudity and disregard for the law were two features in the history of the small town where the Scurlock family resided. And these were two traits that William Scott Scurlock would later embrace.

On March 5, 1955, elementary school teacher Mary Jane Scurlock and her husband, Baptist minister William "Bill" Scurlock, gave birth to a son they named William Scott Scurlock. Scurlock grew up with three sisters, and despite the family's religious foundation, they didn't have strict guidelines. Scurlock knew the difference between right and wrong—he just didn't care. He enjoyed living what many have described as a "Peter Pan" lifestyle. Like the titular character from Scottish novelist and playwright J.M. Barrie's book, Scurlock was free-spirited, mischievous and extremely reluctant to grow up. Later, FBI agents even found a Peter Pan poster in his home.

In 1974, Scurlock visited Hawaii, where he was reunited with an old childhood friend named Kevin Meyers. Kevin was known as a gentle, sweet man who often fell in the shadows of his more adventurous friend. While Kevin had joked with Scurlock about visiting him any time, he was surprised when his old friend appeared on his front porch. He was even more surprised when Scurlock told him of his decision to move to Hawaii. Kevin received a scholarship to attend the University of Hawaii as a pole vaulter. Like Scurlock, Kevin grew up in Reston, Virginia. His brother, Steve, also befriended Scurlock and eventually fell into a trap that drastically changed his life.

Scurlock became employed by Hawaii Plant Life and Privacy Fences, which was owned by Warren Putske. Putske lived in a large home that he shared with several other tenants. He later invited Scurlock to move into the home. Though he made a decent living working for Putske's company, Scurlock applied for several modeling assignments in order to pay his rent. He also used his charm to get a job at the airport as a lei greeter; he happily kissed and welcomed women to the area. He was living a satisfactory and easygoing life.

Meanwhile, cutbacks at the University of Hawaii left Kevin Meyers without a scholarship and with little motivation to stay at a school he couldn't afford. He soon dropped out of the university and found employment. He also found a place to live alongside Scurlock. The pair found many ways to fill their non-working hours. As kids, they would sneak pies from a local pie delivery truck and even waited for the milkman to turn his back to find a way to wash down the pie. As adults, the men found a banana plantation and stole several bunches of bananas overnight.

One night, while they were out adventuring, the men found a small patch of marijuana hidden in a tomato farm. With no regard to their sleep or rest, the pair stole several of the plants and brought them home, where they promptly stripped and prepared the marijuana for sale. The men quickly learned that a dollar was easy to earn if you had no regard for the law. Sometime later, Scurlock planted a few marijuana plants near his home and hid them among other plants to keep them out of sight. When Kevin discovered this, he wasn't happy that Scott had brought the marijuana so close to home. Putske wasn't happy about this either, and he promptly kicked them to the curb.

Scurlock and Kevin temporarily parted ways. Kevin pursued a career in art and hoped to find a stable lifestyle, while Scurlock continued down a path of destruction. In 1978, Scurlock moved to Olympia, Washington, just south of Seattle, and enrolled at Evergreen State College with the hope of becoming a doctor. He excelled academically; he did well in science, especially chemistry. Due to his experience with selling marijuana, Scurlock knew that selling drugs was easy money. So, with a firm knowledge of chemistry and drugs, he plotted to produce methamphetamines. The accounts of this next part are mixed. Some say that he snuck in through the ceiling of the chemistry lab at Evergreen State College, while others say that he passed security by pretending to be a professor. Perhaps this charming and innovative man used both methods. But regardless of how he got inside, Scurlock did find himself in the chemistry lab with all the items he needed to start a profitable business. He went unseen long enough to buy nineteen acres of land just minutes away from the college. After all, the production of methamphetamines also created a horrible smell and was nearly impossible to hide on a college campus.

Scurlock had several structures assembled on his property. The first was a barn, where he had ample space in which to produce methamphetamines. The second was a lavish treehouse. The Hobbit-like structure was buried deep in the boughs of a few tall firs and cedars; it was the perfect hideout. He banded together with a group of friends, whom he openly referred to as his tribe. They assisted in the construction of the treehouse, which was said to have taken just a few weeks due to Scurlock's heavy 24/7 construction schedule. The treehouse was anything but plain; the final product was a three-story mansion that featured hot and cold running water, six-foot-tall picture windows, sun decks, electricity, a wood stove and much more. The treehouse estate became known as Seven Cedars due to the fact that the structure was wrapped around seven large cedar trees.

It wasn't long before Kevin Meyers rejoined Scurlock and moved into the treehouse, where the two resumed their adventures. Kevin didn't like that his friend was producing and selling methamphetamines, but he needed a place to stay until he found employment. The people who surrounded Scurlock, especially his closest friends, enjoyed the benefits of his money. Scurlock had everything; he had friends and beautiful women who constantly surrounded him, and, most importantly, he had money. Due to his unconventional methods, or perhaps due to his distrust for others, Scurlock buried the supplies for his methamphetamine production throughout his property. He also buried his money in locations that only he knew. Despite his success, Scurlock's perfect life took a stumble in 1989, when his main drug distributor was shot and killed. Scurlock feared death and sensed imminent danger. He promptly discarded everything associated with his drug business and decided that it was time for a new career. Most men check the help-wanted ads when they lose a job, but not Scurlock—he created a job.

Steve Meyers later said that Scurlock mentioned bank robbing as a child. Scurlock believed that he could act like Robin Hood by stealing from the rich, corporate banks and returning the money to those who needed it. With the end of his career in drugs, Scurlock needed easy money in order to maintain his lavish lifestyle. He enlisted the help of an old college friend named Mark Biggins. Biggins was also having some financial troubles and struggling to support his family, so Scurlock hired him to work with the property that surrounded Seven Cedars. Biggins planned one bank robbery with Scurlock; they wore masks, like they'd seen in the movie *Point Blank*. This first robbery was a disaster. Scurlock used Biggins's first name while in the bank, and outside the bank, Biggins flooded the getaway car's engine. After this robbery, Biggins quit—at least for a moment.

With each robbery, Scurlock's disguises became more creative. He began ordering professional-grade makeup on the Internet, and during their investigation, agents even found a makeup studio in Scurlock's barn. Scurlock's disguise included a prosthetic, protruding chin, a false nose and mustache. He even topped the disguise off with a wig. While it may have taken Scurlock hours to apply this disguise, it took him only seconds to remove it and quickly change his appearance. During some of the robberies, Scurlock wore everyday brown shoes, but many times, he wore his signature Converse sneakers. The FBI and Seattle's police department nicknamed Scurlock "Hollywood" for his incredible ability to naturally blend in and go unrecognized.

While Scurlock carried out many of the robberies alone, he usually had a driver waiting outside, and Kevin was still helping by laundering the stolen money in Las Vegas. This laundering made it certain that Scurlock and his associates would not spend bait bills in their hometown and risk identification. In later cases, Steve worked as a lookout, making sure that Scurlock could get in and out of the banks without the police noticing his presence. However, as time passed, the police began to see patterns in Scurlock's robberies. He favored specific banks and certain areas of town. Based on the sum Scurlock received during a robbery, police could tell when he might strike next. Agents figured out that he required around $20,000 per month. If the money was low, he'd soon be hitting up another bank. By mid-1996, Scurlock, Biggins and Meyers had robbed at least seventeen banks in four years. The FBI offered a $50,000 reward for the capture of the Hollywood Bandit. Police believed that he was acting alone, as he was the only one to ever enter the banks.

On a typical, rainy night in Seattle, the threesome struck one more time. It was the evening before Thanksgiving, November 27, 1996, and Scurlock had planned his biggest haul: three banks in one day. His last robbery had occurred around 5:00 p.m. at the Seafirst Bank in Seattle's exclusive Madison Park district. The bank was known to hold $3 to $4 million. The theft didn't go as planned. A teller pressed a silent alarm button, alerting police, and a disobedient customer followed them. The witness was able to provide a vehicle description to authorities. The three suspects escaped in one car and switched over to a white van. However, they found themselves stuck in rush hour—holiday traffic. The delay gave law enforcement time to catch up and surround the van. When the van came to a stop, the trio fired upon the FBI agents and police, who returned fire. Biggins and Meyers were both struck by bullets in their arms. Police learned that Scurlock was driving. By the time the van had stopped for a second time, one man had escaped; the other two fell out of the van, covered in blood. Biggins and Meyers required transport to Harborview Medical Center for treatment. Over $1 million was spilled all over the floor of the van, along with makeup, blood, clothing and weapons. There was only one item missing: William Scott Scurlock.

Wilma Walker and her family were prepping for Thanksgiving when the robbery occurred. Her sons, Ron and Bob, wanted to make sure that their mom's home was safe, as it was within the radius that was being observed for the elusive bank robber. Her home was also located less than two blocks from where Biggins and Meyers had stopped. Ron remembered that his old camper was in the backyard and noted that it could provide a perfect hiding spot. The brothers had also heard about the $50,000 reward and knew how badly their mom needed a new roof on her home. Upon investigation, the brothers noted the camper door locked from the inside, and the curtains blocked peeping eyes. Ron fetched a stepladder and peered inside the camper. Much to his surprise, he spotted a head of dark curls resting on the bed. The brothers backed away from the camper and called 911 immediately.

Seattle police officers, FBI agents and detectives from the Puget Sound Violent Crimes Task Force cordoned off a five-mile radius and surrounded the camper. An OC (oleoresin capsicum) spray training officer who was at the scene emptied two canisters of spray into one of the camper's open windows, but there was no response from the person inside. Moments later, a single shot rang through the air. Officers scrambled for cover while over thirty rounds blasted the side of the camper. Officers were ready for a fight and had prepared to use techniques they had learned from a massive shootout in the 1980s in Miami, Florida, where a hostage negotiation was unsuccessful.

Finally, the officers fired a shot of tear gas into the camper and waited, but there was no response. Protected by gas masks, officers approached the camper, where they found the body of William Scott Scurlock slumped over the dinette. A 9-mm Glock pistol helped paint the picture of his death. An autopsy later revealed an entry wound at Scurlock's chin and an exit wound at his hairline—both were conclusive signs of a suicide. Although several of the fired shots struck Scurlock's body, they were noted to have hit post-mortem. With dramatic flair, Hollywood left this world with a bang.

Six officers filed lawsuits against the City of Seattle, stating that they had suffered significant emotional distress during the shootout. They won the case, and the estate was ordered to pay an undisclosed amount. The court's decision forced the Scurlock's estate holders to sell the estate, including the treehouse.

BIBLIOGRAPHY

Aberdeen Herald. "Earliest Legislator." January 1, 1891.

———. "Wappenstein Denies Charges." June 8, 1911.

———. "Wappenstein to Go to Prison." April 29, 1912.

Anderson, Rick. *Seattle Vice: Strippers, Prostitution, Dirty Money, and Narcotics in the Emerald City.* Seattle: Sasquatch Books, 2010.

Bill of Rights Institute. "Olmstead v. United States (1927)." billofrightsinstitute.org.

Daily Intelligencer. "Asa Mercer Dies in Nebraska." February 1, 1877.

Denny, Arthur Armstrong. *Pioneer Days on Puget Sound.* Reprint, London: Forgotten Books, 2016.

Ellensburg Dawn. "Meeting Governor Stevens." November 20, 1908.

Evening Statesman. "Considine Now in Big Lawsuit." October 26, 1909: 7–7.

———. "Fee from Graham Estate." July 15, 1905.

———. "State to Get Lou Graham's Estate." July 22, 1904.

Justia Law. "Ikeda v. Curtis." law.justia.com.

Kennewick Courier. "Wappenstein Sentenced for Bride Taking." July 28, 1911: 8–8.

Larsen, Rachel. *Mercer Girls: Washington's Struggle to Obtain Women.* Self-published, 2011.

McClary, Daryl C. "Olmstead, Roy (1886–1966)—King of King County Bootleggers." www.historylink.org.

McGirr, Lisa. *The War on Alcohol: Prohibition and the Rise of the American State.* New York: W.W. Norton & Company, 2016.

Meier, Gary, and Gloria Meier. *Those Naughty Ladies of the Old Northwest*. Bend, OR: Maverick Publications, 1990.

Metcalfe, Philip. *Whispering Wires: The Tragic Tale of an American Bootlegger*. Portland, OR: Inkwater Press, 2007.

Morgan, Murray. *Skid Road: An Informal Portrait of Seattle*. Seattle: University of Washington Press, 2018.

Murphy, John Miller. "John Miller Murphy Tells Story of Governor Isaac Ingalls Stevens." *Washington Standard*, October 4, 1912.

———. "John Miller Murphy Tells Story of Mercer." *Seattle Post Intelligencer*, December 31, 1897: 5–5.

Nordheim, Teresa. *Murder & Mayhem in Seattle*. Charleston, SC: The History Press, 2016.

Okrent, Daniel. *Last Call: The Rise and Fall of Prohibition*. New York: Charles and Scribner's Sons, 2011.

Olsen, Gregg. *Starvation Heights: A True Story of Murder and Malice in the Woods of the Pacific Northwest*. New York: Three Rivers Press, 2005.

Pomper, Steve. *It Happened in Seattle: Remarkable Events That Shaped History*. Guilford, CT: Globe Pequot Press, 2010.

Richards, Kent D. *Isaac I. Stevens: Young Man in a Hurry*. Seattle: Washington State University Press, 2016.

Rule, Ann. *The End of the Dream: The Golden Boy Who Never Grew Up and Other True Cases*. New York: Pocket Books, 1999.

San Juan Islander. "Tom Considine Tells the Story of Killing William Meredith." November 21, 1901.

Seattle Post Intelligencer. "Another Whitechapel Raid." July 21, 1889.

———. "The Gamblers at Bay." October 18, 1893: 2–2.

———. "Henry Kierski Disappears." April 12, 1890: 6–6.

———. "John Considine Does up Mercury." February 12, 1893: 8–8.

———. "One of the Mercer Girls." August 13, 1890: 5–5.

———. "The Pugilistic Statesman." October 20, 1893: 5–5.

———. "Removing the Dead." August 22, 1884.

———. "Victim of a Syren." February 21, 1890.

———. "Whitechapel Women Win." February 21, 1891: 2–2.

Seattle Republican. "Charles W. Wappenstein Convicted." July 7, 1911.

———. "Sullivan and Considine." December 27, 1912.

———. "Wappenstein Must Go to Prison." March 22, 1912.

Seattle Star. "Ankeny Wins." April 24, 1903: 8–8.

———. "Another Graft Comes to Life." June 10, 1911.

———. "Another Indictment." July 7, 1911.

———. "Considine Down but Still Fighting." November 2, 1915.

———. "Dr. Linda Hazzard Back in Seattle." October 2, 1919: 12–12.

———. "Ex-Police Chief Shot to Death." June 25, 1901.

———. "Gill Lets Chief Wappenstein Resign." July 28, 1910.

———. "Graft Witness Fixed by Wappy." November 26, 1910.

———. "Hazzard Tries Comeback Effort Recalls Death Curse." July 25, 1922.

———. "Judge Griffin Tells How Meredith Met His Death." July 10, 1901.

———. "May Fire Wappy." September 26, 1910.

———. "Scores Points Against Wappenstein." June 1, 1911.

———. "Snatches His Wife Away." April 19, 1910.

———. "Two Police Officers Held in Whiskey Ring Exposure." March 22, 1920.

———. "Wappenstein Pardon." December 20, 1913: 4–4.

———. "Wappenstein Will Go to Penitentary." March 19, 1912.

———. "Wappy Is Fired; Reappointed." June 1, 1911.

———. "Whiskey Smugglers Face Federal Jury." March 23, 1920.

Speidel, Bill. *Doc Maynard: The Man Who Invented Seattle*. Seattle: Nettle Creek Publishing Company, 1978.

———. *Sons of the Profits, or, There's No Business like Grow Business: The Seattle Story, 1851–1901*. Seattle: Nettle Creek Publishing Company, 1967.

Spokane Press. "Compelled to Release Smooth Crook as Woman Won't Testify." August 3, 1906.

———. "Gill Won't Fire Wappenstein." December 20, 1910.

Tacoma Times. "Company Starved Patients for Money." August 7, 1911.

———. "Considine Broke but Still Fighting." November 16, 1915: 5–5.

———. "Dr. Hazzard Is Growing Weak." April 3, 1912.

———. "Fasting Man Is Sought in Vain by Doctors." April 30, 1910: 8–8.

———. "Glad She Is Going Says Mrs. Hazzard." January 6, 1914: 3–3.

———. "Hazzard Granted Parole." December 18, 1915.

———. "Hazzard Score in Defense." January 23, 1912.

———. "How Williamson Sisters Were Starved at Ollala by Mrs. Hazzard." January 20, 1912.

———. "Lister Releases Wappenstein From Prison Cell." December 19, 1913.

———. "Mrs. Hazzard Is Sentenced to Hard Labor From 2–20 Years." February 7, 1912.

———. "Mrs. Hazzard Must Go to Prison According to Supreme Court Ruling." August 13, 1913: 7–7.

———. "Mrs. Hazzard off to Jail." December 24, 1913.

———. "Supreme Court Hears Hazzard Appeal." February 19, 1913: 7–7.

———. "Theatrical Manager Charged by Police." February 28, 1913: 7–7.

———. "To Decide on Dr. Hazzard's License." July 3, 1912: 3–3.

———. "To Rob Lou Graham." *Tacoma Times*, February 20, 1894: 5–5.

———. "Try Dr. Hazzard for Murder of Patient." January 18, 1912.

———. "Wappenstein Jury Disagrees." June 10, 1911.

———. "Wappy Has His Inning." June 6, 1911.

———. "Wappy to the Pen." July 19, 1911.

———. "Webster's Wife." July 14, 1910: 5–5.

Vickers, Marques. *Historic Seattle Architecture: The Aesthetic Alchemy of Ambiance and Chaos*. Seattle: Marquis Publishing, 2017.

Washington Standard. "Interesting Page of State History." September 21, 1912.

———. "Original Story of Arrival Here." November 29, 1912.

———. "Story of Old Stevens Mansion." January 24, 1919: 3–3.

———. "When a Man Marries." August 24, 1917.

———. "When Washington Seperated From Oregon." September 17, 1915: 3–3.

———. "Yakima Chiefs Stand by Treaty." January 28, 1921: 5–5.

Yakima Herald. "The First Governor." July 18, 1901.

ABOUT THE AUTHOR

Teresa Nordheim is an award-winning author with over fifty published articles and three books to her credit. She works full time as a civilian nurse for the U.S. Army and thrives on researching good mysteries and uncovering hidden gems. She gets her inspiration from such authors as Ann Rule, Gregg Olsen and Stephen King. Check out her other books, *Haunted Tacoma* and *Murder and Mayhem in Seattle*.

Visit us at
www.historypress.com

www.ingramcontent.com/pod-product-compliance
Lightning Source LLC
Chambersburg PA
CBHW060346100426
42812CB00003B/1146